CYCLE OF CHRIST

Johannes Pinsk

CYCLE OF CHRIST

The Mass Texts Interpreted in the Spirit of the Liturgy

Translated by

Arthur Gibson

Foreword by Msgr. Martin B. Hellriegel

DESCLEE COMPANY

New York   Tournai   Paris   Rome

Original Edition: *Gedanken zum Herrenjahr*
© 1963, Matthias-Grünewald Verlag, Mainz

The basis of this book is a collection of articles written between 1954 and 1956, which appeared in the periodicals *Der Christliche Sonntag, Michael, Sanctificatio Nostra, Donum Dei,* and *Petrus-Blatt.* The articles have been revised in the light of current developments in the life of the Church.

Nihil obstat:	Augustin B. Vaughan, S.T.D.
	Censor Librorum
Imprimatur:	Terence J. Cooke, D.D., V.G.
	New York, May 7, 1966

Library of Congress Catalog
Card Number: 66-19225

© 1966 by Desclee Company, Incorporated

Manufactured in the United States of America

CONTENTS

FOREWORD

"There was a man sent by God whose name was John. This man came to give testimony concerning the Light." May we presume permission from the "Eagle-Evangelist" to apply his testimony about Christ's forerunner to another "John," Dr. Johannes Pinsk, forerunner of the Second Vatican Council?

I had the joy of meeting Father Pinsk at the Benedictine Abbey of Maria Laach in the German Rhineland at the time when the "Umberg-Casel" debate was in full swing. Heated discussions were then raging between the two camps of theologians. But the theologian Pinsk remained calm and objective. His clear and intuitive mind had detected in Odo Casel one of the leading pathfinders for a theological renewal, a conscious return to the "ancient fountains of youthful strength" (Herwegen): the sacred scriptures, the Fathers of the Church and the living and life-imparting liturgy. I was so impressed by Dr. Pinsk's knowledge and humility, his vision and love of the Church that, on my return from Europe, I began to read once more a goodly portion of his writings, this time with the personality of Johannes Pinsk standing vividly before my mind. I said to myself: "God be praised for this priest and theologian, this prophet and author, this teacher and pastor. Lord, give us more Johannes Pinsks!"

Anyone who is sufficiently acquainted with his writings will quickly discover the massive "footprints" Pinsk left behind for the Council Fathers to follow with safety. In almost every one of the sixteen "Constitutions and Declarations" of the Council one can find the spirit of "the man whose name was John," the John who journeyed on to eternity two years before "another John" convoked the much needed Twenty-first Council of the Church. Johannes Pinsk is another proof of the wisdom and working of the Holy Spirit who, in due season, calls and inspires men to be forerunners for the *Ecclesia semper reformanda*, the constant renewal of the Church, shepherds and flocks.

At present the Church is in a state of transition, a transition from "winter" to "spring." Needless to say, a certain amount of restlessness and confusion can be expected. But let no one become pessimistic. The renewal—the pentecostal breathing of the Divine Spirit—is already on its way. We may compare the present turbulence to the storms between winter and spring. Unpleasant though they be, they are necessary to cast out the last vestiges of a cheerless winter and break open the fragrant blossoms of springtime.

It is, of course, regrettable that there are people "on mountains and in valleys" who never discovered and realized the force of those mighty liturgical, scriptural, and pastoral currents which in God's providence have been "watering the City of God" during the past five decades and, at the same time, were disposing the Church for the necessary Second Vatican Council. But now that the Council has spoken, some of these unprepared persons have become—almost overnight—liturgical, scriptural, and pastoral experts, so involved in peripheral things that they fail to see the need of the sacred center where the fountains of salvation and life are gushing forth in abundance. The changes in a changeless Church are intended to be bridges to the indispensable center.

If "the spirit of the Council" (Paul VI) is to inflame and transform the minds and hearts of clergy and people then all of us must move prayerfully, studiously, and consistently towards the center, else we are going to witness another kind of externalism followed by the same old dullness and indifference. One is reminded of a passage in the Apocalypse: "And there was given me a reed like to a rod, and I was told: Rise, and measure the temple and the altar and those who worship therein. But the court outside the temple, reject it and do not measure it" (11, 1f.). Of course we need externals. We are human beings, not angels. God forbid that we should ever make light of those externals with which the Church in her love for God's service has adorned "the temple and the altar for those who worship therein." On the other hand, let us not become guilty of an inversion of values. The shell which surrounds and protects the kernel is important, but immensely more important is the sweet and life-containing kernel. After all, "the soul of all reform is the reform of the soul" (Cardinal Faulhaber).

In Spring of 1950 Dr. Pinsk published a booklet entitled *Schritte zur Mitte* (steps towards the center) in which he points out the danger of the periphery on which all too many Christians find themselves in a state of unhappy complacency or complacent unhappiness. Our Christian life remains empty unless and until we find the center. There, and only there can we have our fill. And *the* center is the paschal mystery, the death of the Lord "by which he overcame our death" and his resurrection "by which he restored our life" (cf. Easter preface). By his resurrection the Lord Christ merited for us a "new quality of life," a sharing in his own immortal life, thereby uniting us so vitally and ontologically with himself that we can joyfully exclaim with St. Paul: "I live, now not I, but Christ lives in me" (Gal. 2, 19f.). That is *the* center, the center of all scripture, liturgy, history, preaching, in short, of our entire Christian life. And Johannes Pinsk is "a genuine mystagogue" (Carl Johann Perl) to that center.

I rejoiced greatly when I learned of the decision by the Desclee Company to publish in English the treasures of the man who truly "gave testimony concerning the Light," Johannes Pinsk, forerunner of the Second Vatican Council, mystagogue to the center, kerygmatic preacher, inspiring writer and priest with the heart of the Good Shepherd. Desclee deserves our gratitude for its vision, courage, and sound judgment. But our sincere thanks belong also to the translator, Father Arthur Gibson, who has done a masterly job and "deserves to be called, in a sense, a spiritual kinsman of the author" (Theodor Schnitzler).

It is our hope and prayer that the *Cycle of Christ* will become for all throughout the English-speaking world a wellspring of edification and inspiration and, at the same time, a powerful means for promoting the triple aim of the Second Vatican Council: to increase vigor in our Christian life; to foster union among all who believe in Christ; to strengthen whatever can help to call the whole of mankind into the household of the Church.

Msgr. Martin B. Hellriegel, P.A.
St. Louis, Missouri.

Ash Wednesday
February 23, 1966

Introduction

The texts comprising a Mass in the Roman Missal can be divided into three groups. The first and most meaningful are the readings (epistle, gospel); next come the three *Orationes* (Collect, Secret, and Postcommunion), to which should be added the proper Prefaces and the occasional variations in the *Communicantes* and the *Hanc igitur*; the third group includes the Introit, Gradual and Alleluia Verse or Tract, Offertory and Communion Verse. Extensive transpositions of the individual items within their own groups and of the groups themselves must be admitted to have occurred in the course of the historical development of the Mass text; the result is that today the prayers or other texts assigned to various readings are by no means the same as liturgical sources prove them once to have been. Yet the Mass texts found today in the Roman Missal must even today be admitted to possess a substantial and integral unity. We must make an effort, then, to discover this inner nexus of the various texts contained in a given Mass. This inner continuity is often and in many ways the same as that shown by many Psalms, in which we find often a great multiplicity of impressions, emotions, thoughts and judgments, with many verses apparently in mutual contradiction or at least revealing quite different basic attitudes, but with the Psalm as a whole nevertheless retaining a certain unity and integrity. If the word "lyrical" were not too compromised by evocations of sentimentality, the Psalms and Mass texts could be said to possess a lyrical unity. This unity can be recognized only if attention be paid to the relation of the individual groups and of their individual components.

The primary and crucial formative elements of the Mass text are the readings. In them God speaks to us, no matter what biblical author has recorded the message, no matter what priest reads it out. Epistle and gospel are always and everywhere the word of God, truly and actually "words of eternal life" (Jn 6, 68). Consequently the reading of a passage of the Old or New Testament must never be considered or presented as a mere historical report. It is always a genuine proclamation. Now a proclamation differs from a mere report, account, poem or anecdote in one essential feature: it creates *a new reality*. This is true of every human proclamation, political, juridical or social. It is only upon the *proclamation* of peace that a state of peace intervenes; it is only with the proclamation or announcement of the fact that an examination has been passed or a promotion granted that the individual attains his new rank; it is only upon proclamation of a sentence that punishment or acquittal takes effect. New reality is created in a special way, however, by the power indwelling in the word of God. Thus do we hear in a word of Yahweh: "So it is with the word by these lips of mine once uttered; it will not come back an empty echo, the way it went; all my will it carries out, speeds on its errand." (Is 55, 10f.). For it is the spirit of Christ that streams into the community with the readings of the Mass and truly molds that community if it be receptive and malleable. Therein lies the objective factor proper to the readings in the celebration of the Mass; they determine for the individual feast day or Sunday the spiritual (pneumatic) disposition of the assembly of the faithful.

The individual items of the third group, which we will, for the sake of convenience, call the hymn texts, are not objective proclamations but rather the reaction of the Christian community to the objective proclamation of the word of God and to the sacramental sacrifice of Christ. They are intended to express the sentiments and motivations of the congregation on the occasion of this celebration. Here again any purely retrospective understanding or application must be scrupulously avoided. The situation out of which the verses of, let us say, the Gradual were molded initially, *becomes* the situation of the congregation here and now assembled around the altar. This present congregation is not supposed to think itself back into the situation of the psalmist or the prophet or the children of Israel; rather this present congregation speaks these texts *out of its own heart* and in these texts recognizes and attests its own identity. "Let the mind be in agreement with the voice" (*Rule of St. Benedict,* chap. XIX) and not the converse: "Let the voice be in agreement with the mind"! A vital tension thus arises between the objective word of God and the reaction of the congregation. This reaction need by no means be monotone in its consistency; in the individual passages of a group of texts, quite different reactions can be manifested, so that in the succession of the passages there occurs a genuine pneumatic event, a pneumatic exercise of the congregation.

A very good example of this is provided by the hymn texts for the Sundays of the pre-Lenten season. Compare the profound despairing misery of the Introit with the wonderful tranquility and quiet trust expressed in the Offertory and Communion verse. Here it becomes clear that something has happened in this celebration to the congregation that prays in this way. If these texts in fact candidly express a genuine inner event, then the congregation has really undergone an interior change in the course of the celebration. What has caused this change? Simply the influx of the life that has been proclaimed in epistle and gospel and actualized in the sacrificial rite.

Although the nexus of these passages and their integration with the readings and the rite as a whole are especially clearly discernible on the three pre-Lenten Sundays, this inner unity can be discovered in every Mass text without any forcing of the texts. The only thing that will need to be clarified is whether the entire reading or only one or another of its individual sentences fits into the Mass text. This latter situation prevails, for instance, in the gospel for the feast of the Archangel Michael, which is also used on the feasts of other angels. In this comparatively long gospel passage, it is obviously only the last sentence which is meaningful for the feast in question: "I tell you, they have angels of their own in heaven that behold the face of my heavenly Father continually" (Mt 18, 10).

Between the two groups of texts already treated stands the group of the *Orationes*. They constitute, together with the Canon, the priest's prayer as such in the Mass and thus stand midway between the divine objectivity of the readings and the subjective utterances of the congregation. They can therefore give a more moderate and dignified expression to the often passionate, agitated, exultant utterances of the Introit and Gradual; and they can implore for the Church of God the special fruits of the Mass of the particular day. An element of some importance for a true estimate of these *Orationes* is the form of address used to God and the special attributes and operations of grace ascribed to him and serving as the basis for the petitions presented to him.

There are many, very many ways of developing the Mass text. There is absolutely no need always to begin from the text of epistle or gospel, even though these passages often provide the best starting point. Often it will be advisable to begin with a text which is at first glance insignificant and unimpressive, the more so if this text might present certain difficulties, not just in its literary sense but in its integration into the text of the Mass. On the first Sunday in Advent we might commence, for instance, with the question of the meaning for us here and now of the Communion verse: "The Lord, now, will grant us his blessing, to make our land yield its harvest" (Ps 84, 13). What has this verse to do with communion and more especially with communion on the first Sunday in Advent? Or, again, what has the Offertory of the second Mass of Christmas ("The Lord founded the solid earth, to abide immovable") to do with the sacrifice of the Mass on the birthday of the Lord? Or why and in what sense does the congregation assembled today for Mass exclaim that it sits by the waters of Babylon and weeps, when it remembers Sion (Offertory of the twentieth Sunday after Pentecost)? Or how does the Old Testament sufferer Job happen to get into the Offertory on the twenty-first Sunday after Pentecost? What has he to do with the Christian congregation, with the Mass of this Sunday?

Such texts cannot simply be set aside as meaningless, on the pretext that they no longer make sense for us today. If a head collides with a text and the result is a hollow ring, the fault need not necessarily lie with the text in every case! Nor should such phrases be simply read off mechanically because they are there in the text. They must be taken seriously; such phrases must precisely be taken very seriously. Then they will afford a good opportunity for setting in an entirely new light epistles and gospels whose significance has been dulled by repeated reading and interpretation; the new light will be imparted precisely by the connection of these passages with the rest of the Mass text. The fact is that the constant glossing of the gospel passages can become tiring over a period of several years, while these passages can be given a much richer and more plastic elucidation when they are incorporated into the Mass text, which often lends them quite unusual and immediate significance.

The synoptic coordination of the individual parts of the Mass text does not, of itself, provide a thorough foundation for our meditations on the liturgy. Of just as great, if not greater, importance is the incorporation of the proper of each individual Mass into the always identical sacramental sacrifice. Catechetical instruction in the past has often severely neglected the Mass of the Catechumens in favor of the Mass of the Faithful. There may indeed be some justification from the point of view of moral theology for the assertion that it is not a mortal sin to miss the Mass of the Catechumens, that mortal sin begins only with absence from one of the three principal parts of the Mass of the Faithful. But this attitude is indefensible when it is a question of the liturgical understanding of the celebration of the Mass as a whole, for the liturgy of the word and the sacrificial action must be combined into an organic whole in order to amount to what

can justifiably be termed a celebration of the Mass. The liturgy
of the word is important not only because it is, if properly accomplished, the most manifest expression of the active participation of the congregation; of much greater importance is the particular coloring imparted by the texts of the liturgy of the word
to the always identical redemptive action of Christ, as that action
is "carried on" (Secret for ninth Sunday after Pentecost) in the
sacramental sacrifice. As the charism proper to all sacraments is
the mediation or intensification of our participation in the life
of God in Christ, the essential and always identical action of the
eucharistic sacrifice is the *repraesentatio* of the redemptive act
of Christ. This repraesentatio embraces, independently of feasts
and seasons of the Church's year, the redemptive action of Christ,
consummated in his dying and in his exaltation. Yet even in the
case of the sacraments, there is evidence not only that the one
grace common to them all is being applied externally in various
ways but also that their interior effect has quite different nuances.
There would be no point in having seven sacraments if baptism,
say, could produce the same effect as matrimony, or the sacrament of orders channeled the one divine life into the edification
of the life of man in the same way as the sacrament of penance.
These considerations show the power of limitation and specifica-
tion inherent in the external sign and in the word as part of
that sign. This is clearly indicated in the formula used by the
Council of Trent to indicate how the Body and Blood are rendered present separately under the species of bread and wine:
the formula is *ex vi verborum*. There is a *vis verbi* which, without prejudice to the presence of the whole Christ, yet causes his
body and his blood to appear separately. The same could be said
of the specific effects of the sacraments. It is always the whole
Christ with whom we are united, whether in baptism or in ordi-
nation, but the *vis verbi*—or better, in this case, the *vis signi*
(or *vis sacramenti*) prevents the whole fullness from appearing
to us, revealing to us rather only a segment of the salvific sphere of
grace. And the relation of the texts of the Proper to the sacramental
sacrifice can be similarly understood.

On the surface, the gospel passage of any Mass text is describing a historical fact in the life of Jesus. But every individual historical act performed by Jesus in the course of his earthly life is an integral component of his salvific act, of the redemption which he effected. The words and miracles of Jesus are so many particular revelations of the one great fact that the Kingdom of God is present and proceeding toward its consummation. This integration of the individual event into the total salvific action of the Lord must be preserved in the celebration of the Mass as well. The gospel and the other parts of the liturgy of the word are thus integrally linked to the eucharistic sacrifice. The salvific action of Christ is present in the Eucharist but each feast shows us that salvific action under a particular aspect, derived from what the words of Scripture report in the gospel as a fact and interpret in the epistle in its formative application to the Christian community assembled for worship.

The syntatic historical past of the gospel narrative and of the other texts of the liturgy of the word is converted for the assembled Christian community into *living present* by the supra-temporal semantics of the eucharistic celebration. The stilling of the storm on the lake (fourth Sunday after Epiphany) or the healing of the lepers (thirteenth Sunday after Pentecost) are something more than simple historical details taken from the life of Jesus in Palestine. His parables, like that of the prodigal son, of the good Samaritan, of the wedding banquet of the king, of the workers in the vineyard, are something more than stories told by Jesus in those far-off days; they are his revelation, under some one definite aspect, of the reality of the Kingdom of God. And this reality is mediated for us, the Christian community assembled for worship, by the celebration of the Eucharist: we are the ones who are raised from the dead, healed, comforted, reproved, called to follow him—we who here meet our Lord Christ in the celebration of the Eucharist and hear from him the message of salvation in the modality of its proclamation and interpretation in the gospel and the other texts. Every Sunday has, therefore, its own coloring; this coloring prevails not only in the external literary sense of the texts that are spoken but interiorly as well, because there is, on this Sunday, a different epiphany and ramification of the total action of the eucharistic celebration than on any other day.

A comparison suggests itself from the world of nature. A day in winter is, of itself, exactly like a day in summer. It seems different to us, makes a different impression upon us, because the objectively identical sun is presenting to us a different aspect. Even so does Christ remain always the same in his person and in his action; but that action does not appear in its totality to us here on earth in the signs and words of our individual Masses; rather we experience on each occasion only those segments of it which are mediated by the Propers of the various individual Masses.

The integral link between the liturgy of the word and the liturgy of sacrifice is sometimes immediately evident, as when passages from the gospel are used as Offertory or Communion verse. This is so, for example, in the Masses on the feast of the Epiphany, on the Sunday within the Octave of the Epiphany, on the second Sunday after Epiphany, on the third Sunday after Pentecost, on the feast of St. Andrew. In these cases it is quite clear that our eucharistic sacrifice with and in Christ and our union with him are being accomplished within the framework of what has been said in the gospel passage for the Mass in question. But this nexus is always present, even in the Masses in which it is not expressed so overtly. This bond of union yields unfathomed opportunities and invitations for our loving surrender to the Father in Christ and for our union with Christ.

The Mass texts are not neurotically fearful of repetition nor do they join in the still more neurotic hunt for variety at all costs. Even a superficial inspection of the Sunday Masses reveals among them whole series in which the same atmosphere is created Sunday after Sunday. Compare, for instance, the six Sundays after Epiphany, the first ten after Pentecost, or the series of eschatological Sundays from the eighteenth to the twenty-fourth after Pentecost, to say nothing of the Sundays of Advent and

Lent. The congregation which is continually being immersed in this atmosphere will become acclimatized to this atmosphere by the mere fact of the progress of the Church's year, to a still greater extent and in a more perfect way by the constant recurrence of this series of Sundays in subsequent years. Like a child practicing over and over again the same penmanship strokes or a sports instructor constantly repeating the same exercise, until it becomes second nature, the congregation will be caught up into the soaring verve, the sublime grandeur of the Christian life—the life in Christ—and confirmed in it. This is the necessary and sufficient sustaining foundation of a Christian attitude in all situations.

CYCLE OF CHRIST

CHAPTER I

The Season of Septuagesima
Seventy-day Preparation
for Easter

WHEN THE SONG OF PRAISE IS SILENT

At no other point in the course of the Church's year is there such a shocking break between one Sunday and the next as between the Sundays after Epiphany and Septuagesima Sunday. The whole radiant glory of the festal Mass of January 6 spilled out over as many of the following Sundays as were celebrated as "Sundays after Epiphany." As we celebrated them, we were more and more permeated with the exultant joy at the "rising of the glory of the Lord" in his city Jerusalem, the Church. The phrases and perhaps even the choral melodies are still ringing in our ears: "Sing joyfully to God, all you lands ... Let all on earth worship you, O God ... Worship God, all you his angels ... Sion heard and was glad, and all the daughters of Juda rejoiced ... the right hand of the Lord has lifted me up. I shall not die, but live, and shall declare the works of the Lord ..." In these or similar words the congregations of Christian worshipers have been continually exulting on these last Sundays; and now they accompany the entrance of the priest with the phrase: "The moaning of death surrounded me, the sorrows of hell enveloped me ..." A new season has dawned, dark and foreboding. The Epiphany of the Lord recedes behind the shadows and darkness cast by sin over us and our world in the form of misery and death, conflict and tribulation, error and self-deception. A grim state of insecurity: All indeed were baptized, all ate the spiritual food and drank the spiritual drink, but "with most of them God was not well pleased." So ends the epistle; and the last sentence of the gospel, as so often in the Mass texts, states the same conclusion in a remarkable parallel: "Many are called but few are chosen." A most serious and thought-provoking situation indeed! Not as though the epiphany of the Lord with its radiance and exultation had been a deception; it is and remains a reality, indeed the decisive reality. But the Christian world is not yet ready to look upon that epiphany in all its fullness and immediacy; the Christian world, that is each one of us.

And so this Septuagesima, this seventy-day period, stretches out before us; we must traverse it to the place where our Lord died, so that there we may become partakers of the glory of his resurrection. A time of penance, tribulation and conflict, oriented to transfiguration, just as the contenders in the stadium must exert themselves to win the prize, just as the laborers in the vineyard have to bear the burden and heat of the day to earn their penny: but here the prize is an imperishable crown of everlasting triumph, here the coin is life eternal, gift of a gracious God.

In this period, in these seventy days, the joy of expectation, the hope of eternal glory, must be held in equilibrium with the anguish of expectation not yet fulfilled, the sorrow of continuing imprisonment in the transitory. Neither the joy nor the anguish must be neglected or left out of account, on pain of miscoloring the season; about this there will be much to be said on the succeeding Sundays. It must also be noted that the state of expectant waiting still short of the goal is of a different sort in these weeks than it was in Advent. This difference could perhaps be elucidated thus: The waiting in Advent is like the nighttime darkness which in the ordered rhythm of nature precedes the light of day; there is no real anguish in such darkness, for the break of dawn is already in sight. The anguish and uncertainty of Septuagesima on the contrary is comparable to the impenetrable darkness occasioned during the daytime by natural calamities, and chilling the heart of man with fear. The abysmal chasm that yawns between the Epiphany season and the Septuagesima season makes the darkness of this latter season all the more sinister because the Epiphany was already bathed in the brilliant light of the transfiguration.

In the grieving depression thus induced, the exultant cry of the Alleluia dies in the throat. Not until the rites of the Paschal Vigil will we hear it again. The season we now face is the season when the song of praise is silent; it is the season with no Alleluia. And this tells us something very vital about this season, even though many no longer understand that the absence of the Alleluia is so significant. What exactly does the Alleluia mean to us today, in the Mass and the Office? Often in the Mass it is elided almost into a monosyllable and rattled off again without a pause. Can we gain from such performances any impression of the true meaning of the Alleluia, the great victory cry of the people of God? Where it is absent, therefore, we have a time of conflict, of distress and affliction, which prevents the people of God for the moment from uttering the shout of victory.

The church at prayer—and she should so appear in every priest and his congregation!—is very solicitous for the Alleluia, very attached to it. Only with a heavy heart does she take leave of it. In an Augsburg Breviary from the thirteenth century we read: "Even as the children of Israel in the strange land (the Babylonian Captivity) hung their harps upon the willows, so should we in voluntary contrition silence the Alleluia in the time of our affliction resulting from penance." On the Saturday before Septuagesima there used to be celebrated a "Farewell" Office for

the Alleluia; Psalms, antiphons and hymn all combined to constitute this unique and moving office. A few of the texts will serve
to give us a picture of this rite:

"Remain with us today, Alleluia, Alleluia! Only upon the morrow shalt thou depart, Alleluia, Alleluia, Alleluia! And when the
day (of the resurrection) shall dawn, thou shalt walk thy ways
again, Alleluia, Alleluia, Alleluia!"—"The angel of the Lord go
with thee, Alleluia, and see that all goes well with thee, and
grant thee happy return unto us, Alleluia, Alleluia."

A medieval liturgist has this to say about the way in which
the Alleluia is treated and addressed: "Because we are fond of
it and guard it in the treasury of our heart" and he compares
the Alleluia with "a friend preparing to set out on a long journey,
whom we embrace again and again and whose lips and face we
kiss."

We do not have such texts any more in our liturgy. The only
thing left is an addition of a double Alleluia in the Vespers of
the Saturday before Septuagesima, after the *Benedicamus Dom-
ino*, as a sort of farewell salutation to the parting Alleluia!

Here, then, the question might indeed be raised as to whether
we still have that much understanding for the Alleluia these days.
Will we really miss it in the coming seventy days, for instance
after the Gradual, in the beginning of Vespers and Compline?
One thing is certain: anyone who does not deeply regret the absence of the Alleluia, will not experience the surge of joy when
the Alleluia is intoned anew after the epistle in the Paschal Vigil.
The same holds also for the Gloria which is not sung again on
any Sunday until Easter. In all of this, it is not a matter of mere
words but rather of the proper state of mind and soul. This
coming season is precisely the time when we must come to grips,
more earnestly than at other times, with the temptations that
threaten our life with God in Christ. It is the season in which
we must take ourselves more sternly and strictly in hand than at
other times, so that we may not, in our thoughtlessness, misunder-
stand the good things offered to us in earthly forms, so that we

may not become entangled in externals and so become conformed to the world, that world that is in such a sad and desperate state. Yet with it all we do keep our eyes fixed upon the prize, we do work for the eternal coin; that is, we remain aware of the compassionate mercy of God and resist all temptations to despair because of our sins. Whatever may be the struggle and the temptations of this present time, let the face of God shine upon us, we pray trustingly in the Communion verse, then we will not perish. We call upon the Lord.

CHAPTER 2

Septuagesima Sunday

Anyone stumbling unawares from the last Sunday after Epiphany into Septuagesima Sunday will certainly realize with a shock that he is in an entirely different atmosphere, cold, stormy and threatening. He will feel this way, however, only if he is at pains to express his own innermost feelings in the words of the Church and not to prattle these words unreflectively. The Christian community of worshipers has for weeks been exulting over the epiphany of the Lord. It has summoned mountains and valleys, men and the beasts of the field, the whole of material creation and finally even the angels to regard and admire the charism of the glory of God granted to that community of Christians. For weeks, the Christian worshipers have been practicing this stance. They must be reminded of this once more, in order to be shown what is now their actual state, what has happened to them, when they confess today in the Introit: "The moaning of death surrounded me, the sorrows of hell enveloped me. In my distress I called upon the Lord and from his holy temple he heard my voice."

What can have happened? Certainly the individual seasons of the Church's year were not deliberately so arranged as to involve this terrifying transition. It is becoming a more and more probable opinion that what we call our Church's Year did not originally fill out the entire span of the astronomical year; rather the feast of the Resurrection was inserted into the early part of this natural cycle, the time of preparation for this feast was gradually lengthened, until the actual festal season was made to begin with Septuagesima Sunday, with the Nativity cycle being advanced to precede it. So there is no inner nexus between the last Sundays after Epiphany and the pre-Lenten season. Rather there is a break; but this break as such is not only meaningful but good and profitable.

The congregation must therefore be told that the prevailing mood now is quite different from that of the Epiphany season. This might prove confusing at first, as though the reality of the Epiphany were being called in question. Yet what is happening is exactly what we observe year after year in nature: the sun retains its full radiance but our situation alters from summer to winter, not because the sun is changing but rather because different processes are in evidence within us when the sun is not shining upon us. We are the same winter and summer and yet we are different. So it is also with the Christian congregation which is the same in Epiphany and in Septuagesima. But the manifestation is different: side by side with the radiance of God which fills us and vivifies us, there remains our own misery and wretchedness as creatures of earth. Compare the two Introits: Epiphany, "Worship God, all you his angels. Sion heard and was glad and all the daughters of Juda rejoiced"; and Septuagesima, "The moaning of death surrounded me, the sorrows of hell enveloped me . . ." This juxtaposition, in which the same community of worshipers stands and expresses its interior substance, is evidently the key to a Catholic understanding of the Lutheran formula, *Simul peccator et justus.* The attention of the congregation will have to be drawn to this, even if no reference be made to the Lutheran formula.

Whenever and however the texts of this Mass may have come into being, they were certainly not invented in the conference rooms of a Liturgical Commission; rather they grew out of terrible affliction, such as men have themselves experienced in nightly bombings and in the horrors of the encounter with a brutal soldiery. Perhaps it was the restless age of the barbarian invasions, of the irruption of the barbarian hordes into the approaches to Rome and into the Roman Christian community itself, which first brought priest and congregation together in such a cry to God.

This should not be forgotten today. Even today, priest and congregation should unite with all their hearts in this Introit. For what is here expressed is the universal anguish of the Christian world, the Christian world that can, on the one hand, reveal to the angels the secret of the glory of God inhering in the creature, but is compelled, on the other hand, not only to fight the powers of this present world but also to put on the whole armor of God so that it can resist the crafty assaults of the devil; "for it is not against flesh and blood that we enter the lists; we have to do with princedoms and powers, with those who have mastery of the world in these dark days, with malign influences in an order higher than ours" (Eph 6, 10–12).

This is the situation of the Christian community, at all times, even in the Epiphany season; but this situation is especially obtrusive as the congregation stands before God on this Sunday. It is interesting to observe how the congregation copes with this situation. The radiance of the Epiphany flashes out even in the Introit, despite all misery and anguish, in the Psalm verse: "I love you, O Lord, my strength ... my refuge and my deliverer"; but in the Gradual the somber lamentations die away entirely and the concentration is entirely on the help of the Lord who will not always forget the needy, so that the patience of the poor shall not be in vain. In the Tract also there echo the comforting passages of the Psalm *De profundis* which culminate in the avowal that those who are being afflicted for the sake of the Law (that is, the Covenant with God) are resolved to stand fast and endure.

The next corporate manifesto, if we may so express it, is the Offertory, which bears no trace of the anxiety and misery of the Introit: "It is good to praise the Lord and to sing to your name, O Most High." And then there is the last corporate manifesto of the Communion verse: "Let your face shine upon your servant ... Let me not be put to shame, O Lord, for I call upon you." We ought really to be speechless with amazement at this evolution in the community of Christian worshipers during this hour that has been devoted to the celebration of the Mass— always provided that the texts from Introit to Communion verse have not been simply mechanically muttered by pastor and congregation alike! A community of worshipers has changed its posture before God. Into the anguish that cries out of the Introit there shines at the end the transfiguring light of the face of God. Here is a prayer in which something really happens to the worshiper who prays it, as should indeed be the case with every prayer. Something happens to the individual worshiper or to the community of worshipers because they have had a real encounter with God.

This encounter with God occurs in the Word of God and in the sacrifice of Christ. Let us take a closer look at the epistle, the often quoted "sport epistle," sometimes used to provide a justification from revelation for sport, indeed for a Christian sort of sport! In the context of the whole Mass globally considered such thoughts do not arise; but there do come such thoughts as follow from the passage cited from the Letter to the Ephesians, whether it be a question of running or of boxing. We hear but one message: the Christian life does not run its course upon the sunlit meadows of the Epiphany; it is a hard struggle with much groaning and tumult. Yet at the end lies the victor crown for all eternity for those that really live from baptism and the spiritual food and the spiritual drink, even though there always hang over their head as a solemn warning the words, "Yet with most of them God was not well pleased."

The gospel is less somber but here too there is much said about the arduous work which the individual is called upon to perform. The effort and the production output of the individual workers varied greatly but ordinary wage scales do not apply here. It is just as absurd to use this gospel of the laborers in the vineyard as a basis for wage negotiations by Christian trade unions as it is to make the epistle of this Sunday into a sports epistle. The sole real meaning lies in the one coin, the coin of life eternal, which parallels the victor crown of eternity in the epistle. But the words "Many are called but few are chosen" apply to all who work in the vineyard of the Lord; and these words parallel in meaning the last sentence of the epistle. In the gospel, we have the householder who may reverse entirely the normal procedure and give the last the same wage as the first. This is the glad message of this passage. In it we hear the Lord who has summoned us into the anguish of the Introit, the Lord to whom we look up in the Offertory as we declare: "It is good to praise your name . . ." In it we see the Lord who accords to us in very truth and reality in the eucharistic celebration not only the light of his countenance but the fullness of his life in his own body.

Thus does the Mass of this Sunday embrace the whole paradox of the Christian life; it is this which the preacher must proclaim, it is this he must bring the congregation to understand and to experience in faith: that we are not lost when the radiance of the epiphany fades away and the darkness of this age, of this world, covers us. For Septuagesima Sunday already points the congregation to the light of Easter, faintly prefigured and hinted at by the Communion verse of this Sunday's Mass.

CHAPTER 3

Sexagesima Sunday

This Sunday's Mass begins in still more agitated fashion than last Sunday's but its further development is basically the same. The Introit is one of the wildest cries of the Christian community of worshipers to God to be heard in the whole course of the Church's year: "Awake! Why are you asleep, O Lord? Arise! Cast us not off forever! ... Our bodies are pressed to the earth. Arise, O Lord, help us and free us!" We are not used to speaking this way to God; the saccharine tone of modern prayers has made us forget these primordial cries of the human creature aware of his creaturehood before the almighty and unpredictable sovereign majesty of God. Here again training is needed if the community of worshipers is to speak so passionately out of its abysmal anguish to God; for this passionate outcry issues not from unbelief or refractory defiance but rather from the ultimate trust that makes the congregation certain that, despite appearances, God is in fact its refuge and its lord and defender. The congregation of worshipers knows this because it has heard it with its own ears, when "our fathers have spoken to us," have told how God is the God who is always there (*Yahweh*) in Israel's hour of need, as savior and deliverer. But there can arise situations in which the cries of desperation drown out the words handed down from the fathers and in such situations the congregation bellows at God—if we may so express it—yet this very bellowing is a confession that they belong to this God.

Certainly this Mass like that of Septuagesima was born out of the anguish of war and can perhaps best be understood in the midst of the anguish of war and terror of the atom bomb. But even without this, the Introit still retains today its own power of witness to spiritual realities. Witness the epistle, this magnificent excerpt from the second Letter to the Corinthians, flashing scene after scene before our eyes like an adventure film. This reading ought to be made really vivid for the congregation so that everyone really feels for once how a man, not a wicked man at all but a man called to the service of God, can be tormented by God in this earthly life. It is a sheer unending litany of interior and external afflictions, of sufferings inflicted by the powers of nature and by the brutality of men. And again and again beats the persistent refrain: "Perils ... perils ... perils ... perils. .. perils." There seems no end to these perils; and they are so realistic, these perils on journeys through the desert, perils from robbers, perils from compatriots and—O, how close to home this hits even in our own day!—perils from false brethren! How many of those to whom we are preaching this Sunday may well nod agreement that they have experienced just such perils in their professional, civic and perhaps even ecclesiastical life.

They must all realize that in these phrases of Paul is concentrated an immeasurable anguish and affliction, such as very few individuals in our day have suffered in its totality. Yet the man who can document each and every one of these tortures is in the grace of God, and the darkness of his life seems to be lightened when he speaks of the mystical favors granted him. Unutterable secrets were confided to him which—unlike many modern "revelations"—a man may not repeat. But even as this radiance of mysterious exaltation and supernatural happiness begins to transfigure this tragic life, the ultimate anguish flares up, worse than anything recounted in this litany of woes: the messenger of Satan, goading this holy and sanctified man like a thorn in the flesh, buffeting him rudely. This is the state of the saint in which he bellows at God, as in the Introit Psalm. And the only answer he receives from God is, "My grace is sufficient for thee." That is the sole word of comfort in this wild, exciting story of today's epistle. The cry of the apostle and the word of the Lord point beyond mere earthly indigence and anguish to the anguish of man's fallen state, to the lurking malignancy of sin. The question is whether the congregation on hearing this epistle will recognize this anguish as *its own* (even though much less intense) and will realize that it can be healed only by the trusting acceptance of the word of the Lord, "My grace is sufficient for thee, for strength is made perfect in weakness." This will bring the community of Christian worshipers to boast of its own infirmity even as it endures earthly, human and demonic affliction; for it will feel in the endurance of these miseries the indwelling of the power of Christ.

Thus, too, it is clear that the congregation has been changed by the simple hearing of this epistle. Their bodies are no longer pressed to the earth; rather, "Let the nations know that you whose name is God, alone are the Most High over all the earth. O my God, whirl them about like chaff before the wind! You have shaken the earth, O Lord and brought it into confusion [yes, the Lord and not the atom bomb manufacturers has done this]; repair the cracks in it, for it is tottering; that they may flee out of bowshot; that your chosen ones may escape."

This is a palpable example of the formative effect of the word of God, rightly proclaimed and rightly absorbed, upon a congregation, not directly influencing moral decisions but certainly molding the overall attitude.

Thereupon follows the gospel: the parable of the seed that fell on four different sorts of ground. This is first of all an example proving that Jesus did not recount parables, as we do in modern pedagogy and many preachers do in their "pulpit lectures," in order to make things easier to understand. So far as the understanding on the part of the disciples went, the parable was a total

failure. They grasped not a whit of Jesus' meaning.[1] But he explains it to them because to them it is given to know the mysteries of God. And so they discover the fate of the word of God
and consequently of their own activity. But however much the
word of God and consequently also the work of the herald of
that word may be trampled underfoot in the traffic of the world,
there is always at the end the "good ground" of the hearts of
those who keep the word of God rightly and well and bear fruit
in patientia. This conclusion of the gospel echoes the last words
of the epistle: "My grace is sufficient for thee." *Patientia* is not
simply patience, as we understand patience in civic and social
life; rather it is the "spiritual carrying power" (*hypomone*) which
enables human nature to endure the burdens from within and
without and to overcome them through the indwelling power of
God.

We are therefore not astonished at the Offertory song with
which the community of worshipers initiates the eucharistic sacrifice: This community knows that its steps will not falter but remain steadfast; God will work upon it the miracles of his compassion, even though the external symptoms of affliction and
distress persist. Thus, the word of the Lord in epistle and gospel
has prepared the congregation to initiate the sacrifice of the Lord
and that same community that was bewailing in the Introit that
its members had their bodies pressed to the earth stands erect

[1] This is the more remarkable in that Jesus had not told the parable simply
in a vacuum, just for the sake of composing a parable; he had interpolated it
into the quite concrete state of perplexity of his band of disciples. "Why is
he not having the big success we expect? Why do his words and his deeds
not spark the great irruption of the Kingdom of God?"—such were the questions circulating among the disciples and precipitating inner anguish and
crisis. These questions Jesus answers with the parable. The crowd does not
understand it and neither do the disciples until the Lord explains it to them.
This can be the starting point for the application to the concrete situation of
each individual Christian community which cannot understand whence come
the defeats and reverses of the Kingdom of God. Significantly, the first who
falter and fail are the "shallow," a category of Christians who are a frightful
burden for the Church in general and for the individual parish in particular
and yet are shown far too much consideration with the devastating motto,
Fit the standard to the man!

in all its youthful strength and integrity, for it is in the presence of its God "who gives strength to [its] youth."

Such is the stirring Mass of Sexagesima Sunday, in which the congregation of the faithful is shaken to the core but also consoled to the innermost recess of the heart. It is a Mass which always exercises a meaningful and important formative influence on any congregation, if it is properly celebrated.

CHAPTER 4

Quinquagesima Sunday

The community of worshipers begins the Mass of this Sunday with greater trust in God and much more tranquility. We are already more or less familiar, from the series of the Sundays after Epiphany, with the strains that resound in the Introit: "Be a God of protection to me, a place of shelter to give me safety. For you are my strength and my refuge; for your name's sake you will lead me and nourish me." Yet the background of this Introit is still the anxiety and misery of a time of affliction. But we may assume that the congregation has matured. The Communion verse of Septuagesima forms what might be called the foundation for the Introit of Quinquagesima. The whole situation has shifted somewhat. This is shown particularly in the epistle, in which the Church proclaims to us the famous hymn to Christian love. This passage from 1 Cor 13, has been often enough misinterpreted in sentimental fashion. But a closer inspection reveals terrifying images of the futility of man in the order of nature, as Karl Rahner once said.

The opening verses (1-3) contain positively spectacular statements about the capacities of man: they tell of men who possess the supreme gift of verbal expression, whose prophetic insight enables them to know all mysteries, whose power of faith is so strong that they can move mountains; they proceed to speak of men whose passion for self-sacrifice is so great that they distribute all their goods to feed the poor and consume themselves in the service of others. Are these not impressive accomplishments? Are these not splendid human beings, calculated to rouse the admiration of the entire human race? But even as we are ready to stagger in admiration and enthusiasm, we hear the annihilating judgment of God upon these prize specimens of humanity, we hear of their endemic futility: they are a sounding brass or a tinkling cymbal, they are but a cipher; all their accomplishments are of no avail to them—if they have not love. What is meant by this love? Is it the humanitarian sentiment of the researcher and the doctor? Is it personal sacrifice for the community? Is it unstinting generosity to the poor? Note well that all these sentiments are predicated of these persons here mentioned and yet they are said to be nothing! Thus are those whom men call heroes exposed in the futility of the order of nature.

But then Paul speaks of Christian love and—remarkably enough, if you look closely—his first remarks are by no means about the great feats and accomplishments of Christian love; rather he speaks of what that love can bear, what it can *endure*. Verses 4–7 make fifteen statements about Christian love; of these statements, only three are unqualifiedly positive, all the rest being negative. Love in the Christian dispensation is patient and long-suffering: it sustains pertinaciously the demands made upon it. Christian love does not claim its rights: it is not perpetually pushing a zealous assault for position. Christian love cannot be provoked and does not brood over an injury, accepting thanklessness and refusal of recompense or even deserts without further ado. Christian love finds no pleasure in wrong-doing.—These are only a few of the statements which conclude with the comprehensive definition: "Christian love endures all things" (v. 7). A closer inspection of all these statements will show them to be quite insignificant in comparison with the statements in verses 1–3. The feats ascribed to Christian love have not the slightest element of heroism in them; they represent, so to speak, the behavior of the "little people" in their everyday misery. And that is the crucial point for the congregation on this Sunday.

This Christian love is not a human "virtue" nor yet a human accomplishment; it is a supernatural gift, a charism of God. It constitutes the state of affairs we know from the Christmas gospel, of men who are God's friends, men with the love of God in their hearts, who base their concern for and action to relieve the need and misery of their fellowmen upon this love of God—and emphatically upon the love of God and not upon any welfare mentality or purely human "apostolate" of love—; who live in union with God and whose outward operations proceed from that union. These men are transported beyond faith and hope until they feel, in their loving union with God, how trifling are all those things, be they great or small from the human point of view, which might make life hard.[1] They abide in faith, hope, and love, and know that the most abiding and greatest of these three is love.

[1] In the practical pastorate, these Sundays often see the exegesis of Scripture somewhat slighted because of the necessity of reading the lenten pastorals on at least one such Sunday. It might not be a bad idea for the most reverend bishops to reflect whether the words and thoughts of their lenten pastorals can hold their own against such an epistle. This question needs to be posed frankly for once because the pastor in the field—I speak from fifteen years' experience—is repeatedly put in a difficult position each time he has to read a lenten pastoral on such a Sunday. Certainly a way out can be found by the pastor who loves these Mass texts and wants to communicate them to his congregation at all costs; the situation is rendered even more manageable when the pastoral is printed in the diocesan paper. Incidentally, I would like at this point to mention a tactic which is no more armchair invention but has been tested in practice for fifteen years. Suppose you have gospel or epistle passages which cannot be exhaustively treated in a *liturgical* homily, because of the limitations imposed by the necessity of linking up the individual texts. In such an event, an announcement should be made, not in the parish announcements but rather in the sermon itself, preferably at some high peak of interest, to this effect: "Limitations of time unfortunately make it impossible for me to explain the whole meaning of this passage of Holy Scripture; but this afternoon at the afternoon devotions I shall discuss in detail this text which is so important for the shaping of the Christian life. I would be happy if the love for the word of God would prompt many parishioners to take part in the afternoon devotions. It would be a good idea to bring along a New Testament." I can say from personal experience that attendance has been extraordinarily good at such afternoon devotions which precisely offer something more than "rosary and benediction." An indispensable prerequisite, however, is that the pastor prepare very carefully for such a Bible Instruction and be able to do more than parrot a stale paraphrase of various commentaries. This sort of Bible instruction costs a great deal of work, if one is not used to giving talks of this kind; but it is worthwhile, especially if one can clarify details from Old or New Testament history and thus render these details concretely accessible to the congregation of today.

Their jubilation in Gradual and Tract is therefore as great as if it were Epiphany. And indeed the incisive description of the abilities and capacities brought to man by the love that comes from God is enough to open the eyes of their souls to the glory of the Lord: "You are the God who alone works wonders; you have made known your power among the nations. With your strong arm you have freed your people, the sons of Jacob and Joseph. Sing joyfully to God, all the earth; serve the Lord with gladness ... He made us, not we ourselves; and we are his people, the flock he tends" (Gradual and Tract).

But what has become of that people that began this Mass with a plea that had overtones of lamentation despite its restraint? Will the pastor succeed today in so proclaiming this epistle that it will move to such expressions of joy and jubilation each member of the congregation no matter what their individual anguish, need or affliction? Well, I must keep repeating over and over again that this is the whole point of Christian preaching, the aim of this Sunday's Mass.

The gospel takes the same line. The Lord speaks plainly to his twelve disciples of his imminent sufferings. He conceals nothing from them. He tells them the entire story including the resurrection. But they do not understand him. Will we understand the Lord when he speaks in this way to us? Will we understand our involvement in his shame and suffering in the light of the resurrection, still fifty days off? Our sight is also confused by the earthly perspective. Like the blind man on the road to Jericho, we cannot see; but that blind man at least prayed, "Lord, that I may see." Jesus restored his sight with a specific reference to the power of faith: "Thy faith hath saved thee." And so he saw and followed Jesus and praised God. Did the disciples, to whom the words of Jesus concerning his sufferings had remained a dark mystery, understand the sense of this miracle of the opening of the eyes? At any event, they would have joined the entire onlooking crowd as it gave praise to God.

And the community of worshipers here assembled? Has it

grasped the sense of the miracle as connected with the imminent Passion already predicted? The liturgy indicates such a possibility to us in the Offertory: "... Lord, teach me your commandments. With my lips I have pronounced all the judgments of your mouth." It is in this universal surrender to the divine plan which contains so much that is dark and inexplicable for us as well, including the very anguish and suffering of which the congregation was afraid in the Introit; it is in the surrender to these mysterious dispositions and ordinances of God, that the sacrifice of the community of worshipers is today vivified and interpolated into the Passion of Jesus Christ to culminate in the promised resurrection.

The congregation can therefore cast its mind back, in the moment of the reception of the body of the Lord, to the mighty deeds of God which he did to the fathers and this present congregation can be aware by faith that something even greater has happened to it in this Mass: the lamenting community has been filled, its longing satisfied in the union with Christ, and no one has been cheated of his desires (Communion verse).

Once again, what a wonderful transformation of a Christian community of worshipers through the power of the word of God and through the transformative capacity of the sacrifice of Christ!

CHAPTER 5

First Sunday in Lent

ENVELOPED IN THE COMPASSION OF GOD

Anyone capable even to a slight degree of reading aright the text of a Mass and grasping its composition, so to speak at first glance, will be instantly aware of the uniqueness of this Sunday's Mass and will thus realize its most intimate concern and its meaning and importance for the community of worshipers. This Mass of the first Sunday in Quadragesima seems to be unique inasmuch as all the congregational texts are taken from the same Psalm 90. The worshipers wrap themselves, as it were, in the words of this Psalm, they wind the pictures and phrases of this Psalm like cloths around head and body and so stand, robed entirely in this Psalm, before the God they have come to worship. But being robed in this Psalm and standing before God in such a robe means nothing else than standing in the infinite compassion of God which suffices for every possible situation. For Psalm 90 is the classical Psalm of the mercy and compassion of God.

This leads to the question: Why this exclusive stress on the compassion and mercy of God at the beginning of the lenten season? In this Mass of the first Sunday in Lent, during which the organists like so well to play "O Sacred Head surrounded," or other fine hymns of the Passion, the congregation assisting at this holy sacrifice is not thinking of the Passion of Christ at all; rather the congregation has from the outset, in the Introit, placed itself under the sign of God's word of promise: "He shall call upon me and I will answer him...I will glorify him and will satisfy him with length of days." How does this fit together? Something is irregular here. Either the Church is praying off key or the organist has, perhaps together with the pastor, chosen an unsuitable hymn, which would be no unusual occurrence. What place has the compassion and mercy of God on the first Sunday of Lent? The question becomes still more urgent if we cast a glance into the breviary where the same Psalm 90 plays a key role likewise in the ferial offices. Our first thought might be that we have here a continuation of the thoughts and cries of anguish from the pre-lenten Sundays; and perhaps we would not be far wrong! But a more crucial point seems to be the reference to the *catechumens,* who registered in these days on the official list of candidates for baptism, and to the *community doing penance.* For baptism and penance repeatedly signify in practical life a dying, a holding aloof from the vital powers of this earth. It is not for nothing that the general penitential practices are abstaining from food, foregoing sleep and refraining from sexual intercourse in marriage. Even today there are many references to these things in the liturgy. These renunciations include a repudiation of those powers that are the foundation, sustenance and cause of the propagation of earthly life. Anyone trying to achieve an honest repudiation of this sort may be visited by a certain fear of extinction such as visits the one taking a week-long hunger cure for reasons of health.

The catechumen who registered on the baptismal list must have been aware that he was thereby burning behind him all bridges to his old economic, social, familial and civic life. Any day he could be denounced, arrested, killed. He was hanging, so to speak, in the air. And now the Church speaks to the catechumens about the merciful compassion of God in those wonderful concrete phrases peculiar to Psalm 90. These phrases pursue the worshiping community throughout the entire Mass; we find them in Gradual, Tract, Offertory and Communion verse. In these Psalm verses, a prophetic pastor is speaking to himself or to his own and telling what God will do for them. The question arises as to whether the praying priest and the praying community of the twentieth century still take these assurances of God seriously. If not, then this Mass has been a hopeless failure and cannot really be rescued in its true reality even by "O Sacred Head surrounded"; it will become a simple meditation on the Passion.

Side by side with the phrases spoken in assurance to human beings by the prophetic pastor, the Psalmist, God himself speaks to the soul of the praying Christian. It is with the words of God that the Mass begins. We should endeavor to draw the congregation into this conversation with God until it becomes vitally involved, hears what God is saying and gives him an affirmative reply. The community can learn this in gospel and epistle from the two figures which, in these Scripture readings, show us what is meant by this season of Quadragesima.

Paul, the chosen apostle of Jesus Christ, reveals to us the anguish of his own and of our being. We ought not to pause too long over the initial words of the epistle about the acceptable time and the day of salvation on which God hears and helps us. This is the time when we ourselves "conduct ourselves as ministers of God" in all the miseries which Paul again lists in litany form as on Sexagesima Sunday and which we in turn want to present concretely to the community. Here the paradox becomes still stronger. On the one hand, there appears the man pictured in the epistle in all his misery and wretchedness, on the other hand the same man appears in the wealth and riches of the glory of God. The final sentence of this epistle must be unforgettably impressed upon the congregation: we are "as having nothing yet possessing all things."

It seems to me such a phrase ought to be honestly inspected and investigated for once. The initial astounded reaction would certainly be: Is it possible for a person to have nothing and possess all things? Is this not merely an empty phrase, a flight into religious fantasy? The preacher cannot be too drastic in crystallizing the difference between the one who has nothing and the one who possesses everything, so as to lead his congregation gradually to the recognition that this word applies to them, hits their own situation right on the money. The newly baptized who goes to prison: is he free or not free? He is free, unless the freedom of the children of God is but an imaginary phantom and no solid reality. And the martyr who sacrifices his life, pouring it out with his blood—does he die or live? He lives if there is a true life with the risen Christ. And finally, the Christian who possesses nothing more whatsoever on this earth, who has been totally stripped and dispossessed so that he can truly call nothing more his own—is he unpropertied or rich? He is rich if the communion with Jesus Christ also includes a participation in the fullness of his life. Neither God nor the risen Christ is ever poor, ever trammeled, ever dead; and so whoever is united with God through the risen Christ cannot in the crucial and real sense of the words be either dead or trammeled or poor. The community of worshipers must learn to admit for itself the possibility expressed in the sentence, *we have nothing yet possess all things.* It sounds like a splendid answer by the congregation to this last sentence when the community of worshipers begins the Gradual: "God has given his angels charge over you, that they guard you in all your ways." And each succeeding verse of Gradual and Tract does but confirm this integrity and security which is the blessing of the one who calls upon God and surrenders to him.

The message of the epistle is brought out still more clearly in the gospel: the Lord in the wilderness, in horrible loneliness, without any food, with no chance to act and produce results, to unfold his power, the power that was promised to him. And over against him stands Satan, who can dispose of all the things the Lord lacks, Satan who positively preens himself upon being able to procure for the Lord what the Lord does not have. What a horrible confrontation: the Lord as the weak one, the failure, the powerless one; and Satan as the one who provides food, wins over the masses, distributes the kingdoms of the world. Thus it is that they confront one another. And so does Satan confront the Christian community in its powerlessness, its helplessness and its poverty, and make his tempting propositions to it.

It would far exceed the bounds of this meditation to measure the temptations of the Church by Satan against the temptations of Jesus by Satan. Such a comparison would bring out points by no means pleasant for many Christians, highly placed and humble alike. But the final sentence of this horrible picture of Satan vs. Christ shows the victory of the powerless one and it is not just a victory, it is his superterrestrial triumph: "Then the devil left him; and behold, angels came and ministered to him." The conclusion echoes that of the epistle: having nothing and yet possessing all things!

In the sacrifice of the Lord, we enter through him into the most intimate union with the Father. This alone should make us wrap ourselves in the precious, protective and warming mantle of the compassionate mercy of God in all privations and renunciations which time brings with it for the individual and for the Church as a whole.

The goal of this Mass is to bring the congregation to this frame of mind. Psalm 90 must become familiar to the community of worshipers, not only as a piece of superb literature but also as an element fashioning their very life, even when they are compelled to be "in the wilderness" and faced with the apparent supremacy of Satan.

CHAPTER 6

Second Sunday in Lent

THE INVITING GOAL

We could analyze this Mass in the same way as the texts of the pre-Lenten period and those of last Sunday and again find how epistle, gospel and eucharistic sacrifice conspire to raise the community of worshipers to the level of him who is addressed in the Communion verse with such intimacy and fervor as "my king and my God." But we could also take another course which is very rewarding, especially for the interpretation of the Masses of lenten Sundays: we could meditate the picture of Christ in each gospel and do this with special reference to its influence upon the worshiping community of Christians.

The picture of Christ presented in the gospel of the first Sunday in Quadragesima is, humanly speaking, not a particularly attractive one. It levies tremendous demands on individual and community, even if Christ's sovereignty over all human vicissitudes comes out clearly in the final sentence concerning the angels who come and serve him. The picture of Christ presented in the gospel of the second Sunday in Lent, the picture of the transfigured Christ, must have affected the catechumens and ought still to affect us today as an inviting goal. An artless formulation of this power of attraction would be the statement: "That is how we would like to be; that is what we would like to become." And this is precisely what is being expressed by the three disciples present at the transfiguration: they want to build tents, so as to stay here always. This matter of tentbuilding has an interesting background. Building tents and living in them was the Israelites' merriest and happiest feast, the feast of tabernacles, during which the whole thankful people celebrated in Jerusalem the memory of the gracious guidance of that God who brought Israel out of Egypt. It was a feast like no other with its triumphal processions, its temple corteges, its illumination of the entire city, all expressing the joyful expectation of the Messiah; it was a feast on which the hope for the appearance of the Messiah in royal pomp and splendor was expressed in the cries, "Hosanna for the Son of David! Blessed is he who comes in the name of the Lord!" In any case, the three disciples, on seeing their Lord freed from the dust and sweat of this workaday world and standing before them in the radiance of celestial splendor, thought that now the time of fulfillment had arrived for what had been adumbrated by every feast of tabernacles, that the messianic age had now dawned. That was why they wanted to be forever thus with Christ; and, if we understand the report aright, we should also want to exult: "We would like to be forever thus with the Lord." If such an emotion is not produced in the hearts of the worshipers, then it must be bluntly stated that the reading of this gospel has been entirely pointless. Of what possible interest can Christ's transfiguration as a mere historical fact be for us today? But if it be properly understood, then the transfigured Christ emerges as the inviting goal of all those who are detaching themselves from the world in preparation for baptism and in penance. This detachment is a necessary prerequisite, for the transfigured Christ will have no charm or power of attraction for the one who does not detach himself from the world but remains comfortable and satisfied with what the world has to offer. But the catechumens will have realized that this transfigured Christ, the counterpart to the Christ of the temptations, is the fulfillment of all their longing; and this realization will light their eyes and warm their hearts. In the last sentence of today's gospel the Lord does indeed warn the disciples to keep this vision for the time being hidden in secret places of their hearts, until the Son of man be risen from the dead. Only then will his transfiguration be an all-pervading reality. We too must keep this transfiguration for the time being in the faith of our heart; but this must not mislead us into thinking that it has no reality. The hidden is also real!

The epistle instructs us on the point of our own involvement in this transfiguration of Christ: *God's will* is our sanctification, "for God has not called us unto uncleanness, but unto holiness, in Christ Jesus our Lord." The first point here is that the individual is not to be sanctified in himself, in his own actions, but in Christ Jesus. This indicates that here we have to do with an entirely new order of perfection, of holiness which is to be found only in Christ. It is to this kind of holiness and to no other that God has called us. That is his will.

The second point is a very important implication concerning the will of God. I constantly encounter the perplexing tendency of human beings, particularly the most religious, to speak of the will of God only when a major or minor disaster has befallen them. A son or daughter has died: the reaction is abandonment to the will of God, with the remark that God willed it thus. Someone has lost house and home and accomodates to the will of God who willed it. People pray, "Thy will be done" with the interior disposition to accept all adversities, all untoward incidents, all unpleasantness, willingly from the hand of God. This is all very laudable but in the background lurks the thought: Actually it would have been better if things had happened differently, "if things had gone my way"! This is patently not the right idea of the will of God as Paul wants to impress it upon us in this Scripture reading. The will of God is in reality directed to perfecting man in the glory of Christ. Let anyone who has received the body of the Lord, who has been permitted to assist at the eucharistic Mystery, who is living in a state of sacramental matrimony, —let such a Christian just once get the thought: the fact that things have fallen out for me this way, the fact that I am involved in this way in the work of Christ, the fact that I can become

effective in this way in the grace of his redemption—all this is
the will of God. And such reflections would necessarily impel to
the very positive prayer, *Thy will*—the sanctification of mankind
and of the world and of me as a part of both—*be done.*

Thus here again epistle and gospel complement each other.
The epistle may be said to be devoted to the theoretical aspect
of the salvific will of God, while the gospel shows us what this
salvific will of God makes out of human nature, first in Christ,
then in his flock which now, in the mystery of the Eucharist, walks
with him in his ways in loving surrender to his will. It is a curious
and noteworthy point that we find here no protestations of will-
ingness simply to "conform" in pious humility to the commandments of God, which are the integral embodiment of the sanctifying will of God (epistle). Rather the express emphasis is on con-
templative and active devotion to God's commandments *quae
dilexi valde*—"which I love dearly" (Offertory).

Such an understanding of the will of God also spills over into
joy at our being permitted to unite to us in communion the Lord
who so wills our sanctification; joy that he is not only our God
(in the sense of *causa prima* or Unmoved Mover or the aeons-
distant Lord of the universe) but also our king, concerned for
his people's weal and woe. *Salus regis salus populi!* That is the
ultimate foundation of the unutterable fervor and the magnificent
sublimity that cause the hearts of the praying community to over-
flow in the short ascriptive formula, *Rex meus et Deus meus*—
"my King and my God!"

CHAPTER 7

Third Sunday in Lent

EYES ON THE STRONGER

The encounter with Christ is of vital importance for anyone devoting himself to penance and thereby practicing detachment from this world, from the sources and forms of its life, whether it be one who is preparing himself in this way for baptism or one who is already baptized and wants to keep his power of decision supple for everyday life. If any such one loses sight of Christ, then the gaining of the "new" life will have no attraction for him and he will rather be paralyzed by the fear of losing the "old" life, a fear that will haunt his thoughts and inhibit his actions. Thus the lenten Christophany will be a crucial factor in penance properly understood and rightly practiced.

Anyone who has seen the Christ of the temptations in the wilderness, as portrayed by the Mass of the first Sunday in Lent, knows from what things Christian penance will cut him off. Anyone who has seen the transfigured Christ, as portrayed by the Mass of the second Sunday in Lent, knows to what heights Christian penance will raise him up. The transition from that old life to this new one—the true *passover* as we shall see later—is difficult and hazardous, involving the sort of risk taken by the man who lets the sparrow he is holding in his hand fly away before he has his hand on the dove on the roof. What guarantee does he have that he will get the dove on the roof? What guarantee do we Christians now doing penance have that we shall in fact attain to the new life?

In this state of mind does the community of worshipers pray today: "My eyes are ever toward the Lord..." and "To you... have I lifted up my eyes. Behold, as the eyes of servants are on the hands of their masters. And as the eyes of a maid are on the hands of her mistress, so are our eyes on the Lord our God, until he have pity on us" (Introit and Tract).

What a wonderful picture is this play of eye and hand! Just in this way do children stand around the table and stare; hungry they are, to be sure, but they are confidently expectant as they watch the mother's hand cutting slice after slice off the loaf of bread. Although the bread is still in their mother's hand, it has already been "devoured with the eyes," it is already in the possession of the children. Even so do our eyes watch in confident expectation the hand of our Lord!

Is there such a thing as this hand of the Lord? Yes, there is; even if not in the familiar shape of the palm with four fingers and thumb attached, certainly as an efficacious sign of the paternal kindness and the sovereign omnipotence of God. It cannot be otherwise for there are too many mentions in Scripture of the hand of God and, in the same sense, of the arm of the Lord. We ought sometime to make a list of all the things that the hand of God and the arm of the Lord have done and still do. We still pray today: "Thou dost open thy bountiful hand..." Has this protestation become but a too familiar pious phrase or do we really still believe, not merely in God in a general sense, but precisely in the hand of God as well? If we do, then we ought to be certain in our own mind that "the hand of God" is a more potent help than "the arm of flesh," the *brachium saeculare* to which even Christians often prefer to have recourse than to the hand of God. Many still do not understand even today that the dove in the hand of God is more surely in our possession than the sparrow in our own hand. Such people take as their motto:

Don't take any risk as a Christian! Now the opposite of this motto is: Do penance as a Christian!

If we, the penitential Christian Church—from the pope and the whole clergy right down to the babes and sucklings (cf. epistle for Ash Wednesday, Jl 2, 12–19)—if we have, on the basis of such texts as today's Introit and Tract, come really to understand the power of the hand of God and the reliance we ought to place in that hand, then we will be astounded to hear in the gospel that we do not need even the entire hand of God; the "finger of God" alone is sufficient! In that finger of God Christ casts out devils and by it he establishes the Kingdom of God, that living glory that burst upon us last Sunday from the transfigured Christ. It is the Lord, our Lord, who vanquishes the strong, strips him of his armor and divides his spoils. Nothing is lost to us of all those things that belong to the devils as "the strong," nothing of all that they have usurped, nothing of all that we had to leave in their hands when we were doing penance. Our Lord is the "stronger than" they. He takes everything away from them and distributes it to us again, even as he once enabled his chosen people of the Old Testament to gain possession of the treasures of their masters and oppressors at the time of the Exodus (Ex 12, 35).

So too do we penitents gaze upon the Lord in the gospel and see him as "the stronger" who has but to lift his finger to overcome the world. He it is on whom we turn our eyes full of trust and joy; he alone it is who takes from us the fear that we might lose the world and life when we do penance. A mysterious power and grandeur must have radiated from the Lord as he spoke these things of himself, so that even the "certain woman from the crowd" whom we quote so often could have that immediate intuition of this sublime grandeur that was his and begin, like a typical woman and mother, to praise his mother. But just as blessed as she are all those who confide themselves without reserve to the stronger one and the power of his finger. This is the charismatic and consoling culmination of this gospel and of

Christ's gospel as a whole: "Blessed are they who hear the word of God and keep it."

What a perfect promise for those who are in the act of forsaking the world and becoming children of God by the acceptance of the word of God. This Sunday's epistle makes clear to us that this Beatitude of the Lord is meant for *us*. All his admonitions to manifest union with God in the practical life of everyday, Paul bases on the simple fact: "You were once darkness, but now you are light in the Lord. Walk, then, as children of light, for the fruit of the light is in all goodness and justice and truth."

Here we discover ("we" always means the community of worshipers gathered around the altar) what the finger of God has made of us, in plucking us out of the darkness, out of the kingdom of the "strong man" and causing us to become light, whose threefold fruit is comprised by the Christian life. This, then, is our state! And this self-awareness that springs from faith will keep our gaze fixed in unwavering trust upon "the stronger" even as we give up familiar and cherished things in this penitential season. For whatever they may be, the precepts of the Lord, *his* decrees, *his* ordinances are, as opposed to those of the world, our joy and our savory food. And so we confess in the Offertory: "Your servant,"—we, the congregation of worshipers here assembled—observe your precepts; and we confidently apply to ourselves the Beatitudes of the Lord.

Thus do we enter into the sacrifice of Christ in total and unreserved abandon to the Father. And the end of the matter is that we are no longer faced with the choice between the sparrow and the dove. Just as both sparrow and dove are safely sheltered in their own nests, so are we, this very day, this very Sunday, securely sheltered "in the house of the Lord, at his altar" (Communion verse). What a multitude of apparent contradictions are resolved into joyous harmony and exultant thanksgiving at the altar of God: the sparrow and the dove, the advantages renounced and the prize to be gained, the fear of the strong man and the luminous assurance brought by the hand of the stronger—all is absorbed into the calm assurance of sanctuary at his altar, in his house.

In conclusion, a few observations drawn from practice and intended to be of help in practical parish work.

Who would presume to say, after such a Mass, if it is properly understood and rightly celebrated, that the Church's liturgical prayer is cold and has no appeal to the emotions? Does not this genuinely beautiful Mass text in fact truly appeal to the heart and emotions precisely of the simple ordinary folk, not sentimentally to be sure, but for all that in most poignant fashion, so that all of them feel and know themselves to be at home forever "at the altars of the Lord"? And do they not draw this very certainty from the word of God and the Sacrament of the Altar, if they be true believers?

Another point: can well-informed organists be blamed for preferring not to play at this Mass such Passiontide hymns as "O Sacred Head surrounded" and the like? Do such hymns jibe with the attitude and posture of the praying church on this Sunday? Surely the answer is obvious: what a great deal is lost if the integral organic whole formed by the texts of this Mass be suppressed and concealed from the praying Christian community!

If a congregation has really followed this Mass, or better, has really actively assisted at its celebration, and then at the end says: At your altars, in your house, O Lord of Hosts, my King and my God, here is my dwelling-place, here is my home for all eternity!—has not this congregation really and truly become "a people of God"? Are they not a family of Jesus Christ?

These points seem to me to be of importance for every parish in our time that wishes to mold itself into a genuine Christian community. They raise questions which all parish priests ought to discuss frankly and honestly with their parishioners (and perhaps sometimes the parishioners themselves must here take the initiative), to the end that we, the Church, may not receive the grace of this holy season in vain.

CHAPTER 8

Fourth Sunday in Lent

THE SONS OF THE FREE WOMAN

It is not that Laetare Sunday erupts like a sudden and isolated geyser of joy in the wasteland of Quadragesima. The note of joy is sounded before and after, even in the ferial Masses. And how could it be otherwise! We are, after all, marching through Quadragesima toward Easter, toward the Resurrection of the Lord and our own resurrection; and the further we advance, the more does our joy increase. But one thing is true: the community of worshipers is downright overwhelmed with joy on Laetare Sunday, from beginning to end of the Mass.

We, catechumens and penitents together with the community of the faithful, are addressed and greeted as "Jerusalem," as "all you who love her." What is the identity of Jerusalem for us Christians of the twentieth century? Is it the city that was destroyed in the year 70 A.D.? Or is it the city for possession of which even in these days the Arabs, sons of Ismael, the son of the slave-girl, and the Israeli, sons of Isaac, the son of the free woman Sara, are locked in bloody strife? Neither is of any consequence for the eucharistic celebration. "Jerusalem" is here more than a geographically identifiable city. Jerusalem is the symbol chosen by God himself for his chosen people, for his holy city. But it is we who are that people of the New Covenant, the Church of Jesus Christ. We are the true Jerusalem, in the same sense that we are, in St. Paul's words, the true descendents of Abraham, the father of the believers; in exactly the same sense that we are the true

Israel. For unto us have been fulfilled in Christ the promises that were made to Abraham; unto us have been fulfilled, even if still in part in a hidden and imperfect way, the promises of the prophets. We must therefore realize that we are the ones directly addressed in the Introit, addressed by the word of God saying to us: "Lovers of Jerusalem, rejoice with her, be glad for her sake; make holiday with her, you that mourned for her till now. So shall you be her foster-children, suckled plentifully with her consolations, drinking in to your hearts' content, the abundant glory that is hers. Thus says the Lord, Peace shall flow through her like a river, the wealth of the nations shall pour into her like a torrent in flood; this shall be the milk you drain, like children carried at the breast, fondled on a mother's lap. I will console you then, like a mother caressing her son, and all your consolation shall be in Jerusalem" (Is 66, 10–13).

I have here cited the unabridged text from the prophet Isaias, not only because of its very great beauty and the consolation it mediates, but also in order that we may gain a direct appreciation of the maternal and life-giving vitality of the Church as we read its plastic phrases (unfortunately polished into unrecognizable form in the Missal translations). The persistent motif of the breasts of Jerusalem presents to us the Church as a true mother, reveal her in all her *maternal* fullness and power.

The fathers of the Church never scrupled to speak again and again of the maternal breasts of the Church, considering this to be an expressive symbol of the fact that the Church truly nourishes us, even as she has truly given us birth. The primary manifestation of the motherhood of the Church does not lie in the solicitous, sometimes almost anxious admonitions and instructions she gives us. These are secondary, deriving from her primordial function as our mother, in bearing us out of her womb, which is the baptismal font, and nourishing us at her maternal breast. These are no mere vague metaphors. They express a reality which is no whit the less truly real because it lies beyond the boundaries of our natural, physical organism.

The first to speak of the Church in this way was St. Irenaeus:

"Whosoever does not partake of the Holy Spirit shall not be nourished unto life either at the breasts of the Mother (the Church);" that is, the Church mediates in truly maternal love those salvific graces we need in order to be able to live as Christians. Similarly St. Augustine represents the Church to us as she who nourishes us "with the breast of the Faith." St. Ambrose's rhetorical question: "What are the breasts of the Church? Are they not the sacrament of baptism as often as it is administered?" gives the Introit of today's Mass a special significance for the catechumens. The life-giving and nourishing breasts of the Church become for the catechumens auspicious foretokens of their imminent incorporation into the people of God. Just so, the inscription over the church of San Lorenzo in Damaso proclaims: "The portal stands open to all to whom the church proffers her breast."

When we have come to understand this language of the first Christian centuries, we shall also understand what St. Paul means in this epistle and the relevance of his words for today's entire Mass. We are no longer members of the Jerusalem that was founded upon the Old Covenant of Sinai, consigned to the bondage of the Law; rather has Christ freed us from this bondage, by calling us to the New Covenant of the freedom of the children of God. He has begotten us of the "free woman," of the Jerusalem that is no longer under the Law, of the Church whom he has taken as his bride, in all her beauty, without stain or wrinkle (Eph 5, 27). Out of this marriage bond of Christ with the Church, to which nuptials the entire Old Testament was ordered as a preparation, we have been truly begotten as "children of promise," begotten of the free woman who is our mother, begotten to the freedom to which Christ has called us.

How must such words have sounded in the ears of the catechumens! This, then, was their destiny, their vocation! Were they uprooted from home and family? They would find a new hearth and home through the Mother Church among the people of God. Were they to be politically disenfranchised, ostracized? They rejoiced to know that they were on the way to the House of God, to that new city in which there would be peace and prosperity in security (Gradual). And this overcame all those primordial fears that had been engendered by their decision to take their stand for Christ and the Church. Face to face with such a Church, mother of life and city of peace eternal, the catechumens confess in exultant joy, together with the whole Christian community, their ultimate assuagement, the slaking of all their fears and longings: "They who trust in the Lord are like Mount Sion; he who dwells in Jerusalem shall never be moved. Mountains are round about it; and the Lord is round about his people, from henceforth and forever" (Tract).

Whatever the baptized Christian has renounced in his break with the world, he finds it again in the holy city of God, in the shelter and sanctuary of Mother Church. Even so did the prophet Isaias promise in the word of God cited above.

To those who are so eagerly gazing upon the Church, the Lord appears in the Gospel in the company of his disciples. This is a new encounter of the congregation with Christ: after meeting the Christ of the temptations in the wilderness, the transfigured Christ upon the mountaintop, and then Christ the stronger, they now encounter Christ, the giver of life. He orders the disciples to distribute the food. The fullness of Christ is in his Church. He alone it is who makes the Church the blessed mother of the free.

We remember that the Lord was himself once hungry in the wilderness and refused to procure bread by miracle. But today he performs before the multitudes the miracle of the loaves. Yet he has no intention of signifying thereby that he is assuming the duties of a minister of food! This was the idea the people had after the multiplication of the loaves. They wanted to make him king and thereby impose upon him the obligation of providing their daily bread. Christ refuses the proffered crown. What he has done points beyond earthly bread to the food "which affords, continually, eternal life" (Jn 6, 27). Only when he comes to celebrate the marriage feast of the Lamb, only then will he proffer the food of immortality to those who sit at table with Abraham, Isaac and Jacob.

In the face of all this, can we wonder that the congregation enters into the sacrifice of Christ with loud, unbroken exultation, in an Offertory verse which articulates that insight that overcomes all dejection and fear: "All that he has willed, he has done in heaven and on earth"? Can we wonder that the congregation which has learned in this Mass what it means to be the Church, should again break out into loud exultation over "Jerusalem ... built as a city with compact unity," the city in which all find sanctuary and freedom to intone the hymn of praise to the name of the Lord" (Communion verse)?

And so this Sunday should be the true, the original "Mother's Day," the Sunday on which the whole Church rejoices. Are we not desperately in need of such a discovery of the spiritual reality of the Church? Not in the mad whirl and fever of large-scale rallies, at which the world can easily outdo us any day! For, despite all mass demonstrations which Christians may organize, the Christian community must still accept the fact that it is and remains the "little flock" (Lk 12, 32). We should never allow ourselves any false illusions on this point. But this does not mean that we need to or ought to be troubled perpetually by gnawing fear and apprehension. Amid all the vicissitudes and all the insecurity of earthly life we have one ultimate fortress of security that no other community on earth can boast: the certainty that the Father will give us the kingdom through our Mother the Church, who bears us unto freedom and therewith to power, to riches, to glory, to the joy unutterable of the sons of God.

If only we would bear in mind from one Laetare Sunday to the next, from one Lent to the succeeding one, with ever-increasing comprehension, what a wonderful gift it is to be children of the free woman!

This too is a realization Lent should bring to the Christian community of worshipers! And so the observations drawn from practice and intended to help in practical parish work would be exactly the same for this Sunday's Mass as for last Sunday's.

CHAPTER 9

Passion Sunday

BEATA PASSIO

It is true, of course, that the two weeks immediately preceding Easter do belong purely chronologically within the Quadragesima period; but they stand out so drastically in contrast to the preceding period that we give them a special name: Passiontide. During Passiontide, the Church gives preference, as she has not done in the first four weeks of Quadragesima, to the commemoration of the Passion of Christ. But this liturgical celebration of the Passion of Christ has a character all its own. It does not confine itself to recalling to our minds and presenting for meditation the details of the historical Passion; nor is it the intention of this liturgical celebration to recall that Passion only in order to excite in us a melancholy and pitying compassion. The Church is here seeking, just as she did at the Christmas crib, to introduce us in her Passiontide liturgies into the reality of Christ's Passion as part of salvation history.

Consider quite simply the question: What really happened on Calvary? One answer can be found simply in the recounting of the details of the sufferings of Jesus, according to the gospels and Christian tradition, from his arrest to his agonized and shameful death on the cross. This is the way in which we picture to ourselves the Passion of Christ in order to arouse pity and compassion as a basis for sorrow and expiation, as a sign of loving solidarity with the suffering Lord. This is not the way in which the

Church pictures the Passion for us. Look at today's epistle: it tells us that Christ has entered once for all by virtue of his own blood into the Holy of Holies and obtained eternal redemption; he, who through the Holy Spirit offered himself as an unblemished sacrifice unto God, has freed us from dead works by the all-vanquishing power of his blood; in his death, he has become mediator of a new covenant, so that they might receive the promise "who have been called to the eternal inheritance in Christ Jesus our Lord."

These are two very different answers that can be given to the question, "What happened on Calvary?" Both answers doubtless belong together, for the events they report are interdependent. But one thing becomes clear: anyone who stops short at an emotional contemplation of the external circumstances, of the poignancy of the Passion of Christ, is not grasping the real mystery, the *mysterium passionis Christi*. The Church reveals that mystery to us in the epistle, in the lofty words of the Letter to the Hebrews.

It is in the light of the realization of the true nature of that event upon Calvary that the texts of the Introit, the Gradual and the Tract must be understood, as well. They could, of course, be applied to the afflicted Christian community, just like similar texts of the preceding Sundays. Nor would this be in any sense an unjustified or mistaken application; but these texts can only be thoroughly appreciated when they are seen in the light of the epistle, because then the fate of the afflicted Christian community is most closely aligned with the Passion of the Lord and thereby endowed with the power and conquering impetus of that Passion. The followers of Christ, like their Master, are always parrying a faithless people, the deceitful and impious man. This is demonstrated by the history of Israel as chosen people; it is equally demonstrated by the history of Christianity and of individual Christians. The Church and the individual Christian member of the Church are always imperilled by the powers of this world, by sin. But the Passion of Christ shows the happy issue, proclaimed especially by the congregation in the words of the Tract: "Often have they fought against me from my youth. Yet they could not prevail over me. They have contained their iniquity, but the Lord, who is just, will humble the pride of the sinners." If we see this on Calvary, it proves that we have understood the mystery of the Passion of Christ; and if we see this in the hectic vicissitudes of our own lives, no matter what the outward issue, it shows that we are truly united to the Passion of Christ.

That the texts of Introit, Gradual and Tract are primarily to be applied to Christ in the context of this Mass is especially evident from the gospel, with its report of Jesus' splendid debate with his opponents. One would think that modern religious feeling would actually be bewildered by the fact that the Church does not raise the curtain of Passiontide with a lamentation by the Saviour over his Passion (if, indeed, such a lamentation can be found). Instead, Christ tells his opponents, with unprecedented sovereign serenity, of the judgment of the Father, which will favor his just cause; he speaks of the glory that will be conferred upon him by the Father (cf. the nexus with the epistle); and, most of all, face to face with death, Christ speaks of his power, of his eternal life, not only claiming this power of eternal life for himself but ascribing it likewise to those who keep his word: they "will never see death." The band of his opponents is so provoked, indeed infuriated by the imperturbability of his declaration, "Before Abraham came to be, I am," that they take up stones to cast at him. The Christ presented to us on Passion Sunday is a worthy peer of the Christ presented on past Sundays of Quadragesima. Again and again, in the midst of all his anguish and indigence, in the teeth of all challenges and attacks, there shines forth the interior grandeur, nobility and glory of the Lord. So it was that the catechumens and the penitents saw him; so, too, should the whole community of Christians see him today, as they prepare to commemorate and celebrate his Passion.

This solemnization of his Passion which is also a participation in it is achieved even today in the accomplishment of the eucharistic sacrifice. The Christian community has learned that sacrifice is not destruction and extinction, but rather an entry into the Holy of holies and an attainment of the everlasting inheritance; and so the Offertory is no threnody or lamentation but rather this: "I will praise you, O Lord, with my whole heart ... that I may live and keep your words [the same phrase as in the gospel]; O Lord, give me life according to your word." With these dispositions does the Christian community enter with Christ into his Passion which is truly accomplished at the altar, even though under sacramental veils. And if the congregation consummates the sacrificial rite with the sacrificial banquet, then once again there lies before that community the whole grandeur of the fruit of the Passion of Christ: the body that is given for you, the cup of the New Testament, the perfect partaking of the Lord in the rite he prescribed for a perpetual commemoration of himself.

With such dispositions does the Church enter into the solemnization and sharing of the Passion of Christ, with prayer and sacrifice, disclosing to us the profound exhilarating import of the *beata passio*, the blessed Passion of Christ. It is an indisputable fact that any Christian community entering in this way into the Passion of Christ will gain that serenity that Christ reveals in his Passion.

CHAPTER 10

Palm Sunday

IN THE PASSOVER OF OUR LORD

The Church does not call the last week of Lent Holy Week, as we are accustomed to call it; as early as the fourth century and ever since her usual designation, both in east and west, has been *Hebdomada Major*, the Greater Week, the week that is greater than all others. Its greatness derives from the events which will be rendered present to the congregation in the rites of this week: from the entry of Jesus into Jerusalem, through his suffering and death to his lying in the grave and his resurrection. The Church condenses all of these events into the single expression, *Pascha Domini*, Passover of the Lord.

The mere fact that this designation is no longer customary today is no reason not to use it any more. Such a refusal to employ this and other ancient expressions could easily involve a loss of Christian substance, at least in the minds of the Christian community of worshipers. If we trace the etymology of that word *pascha* we shall see that it is an expression which, better than almost any other, transcends even the rites of this week to pinpoint the essence of Christian living.

For the Greek *pascha* comes from the Hebrew *pesach* which designated that first passover of the Lord at the exodus of the Children of Israel from Egypt. Later, the scope of the expression *pascha* was extended to include the crossing of the Red Sea, when the Israelites passed over into the promised land. Canaan was likewise considered as a *pascha*, a transition or, more explicitly, a forward march, a passing onward of the Lord who went before his people, to lead them out of Egypt, the "house of death" and "land of bondage," into the freedom of his own land.

These events were however only foreshadowings of the fullness of the reality still to come. The crucial Passover, which incorporates the whole of the spiritual reality foreshadowed in the historical occurrences, is *Pascha Domini Nostri Jesu Christi*, the Passover of our Lord Jesus Christ from death to life, or more accurately, from life in bondage and lowliness to life in the glory of God.

This Passover is "celebrated" with the congregation in various forms. We might well use here two less modern expressions: this Passover is "kept" or "solemnized" by the congregation. In the notion of keeping a rite, there is evoked a strong note of continuity, for the sense of the rite is always the same. And solemnization evokes the solemnity of a procession, always involved in every festival rite and always having an identical significance. In a festal rite, man is striving after a higher, more exalted level. He wants to have "something different," something more exalted and solemn than anything that workaday life can afford. And this processional route, his route of access, is the rite itself.

This is the proper way to understand the procession of palms, preliminary to the Palm Sunday Mass. What is the meaning of Jesus' entry "into Jerusalem" amid the joyous shouts of the crowds? The cry of *Hosanna!* that rings out during the entry procession was originally a typically messianic cry, the clamor for the messianic kingdom: "Bring good cheer! Bring salvation!" It is the same cry that rang out on the occasion of the great procession at the feast of Tabernacles, in which wreaths of foliage were carried. The multitude accompanying Jesus' entry into Jerusalem evidently adopts the same ecstatic attitude, for Jesus is the Messiah-King, and as such they escort him into the city of God, in which the Kingdom of God is to be proclaimed. Thus it is *Pascha Domini*, the passing, the passover, the entry of the Lord, but an entry accompanied by his people. And that is also the sense of our own procession of palms. The palm branch handed to us makes us participants of the triumph of the King. The olive branch mentioned in the prayers in connection with the palm branch signifies the peace of the Kingdom of God, a peace implying the absolute inviolability of the holdings of the Kingdom of God, an inviolability assured by the victory of Christ. The favored multitude present at the entry of Jesus into Jerusalem in that fateful springtime long ago already grasped what was here being foreshadowed. Redeemed humanity, illuminated by the celestial light of faith, goes out to meet our redeemer, who subjected himself to human sufferings and was about to close in mortal combat with death for the life of the whole world and triumph by his death. That original entry into Jerusalem therefore already transcended the bounds of the purely historical. And when we march today in a procession of palms, we are also entering, together with Christ the King, into the holy Jerusalem, whose transcendent reality is figured forth for us by the House of God. To the victor over death we cry, with the angels and the children of the Hebrews: *Gloria, laus et honor,* "Glory, praise and honor be to you, Redeemer, Christ the King."

This can, of course, all be regarded as a mere ceremony. But it is more. It is a symbolic event, in which we grasp that reality foreshadowed by Christ when he entered into Jerusalem. (This original entry into Jerusalem was neither a historical accident nor yet a theatrical spectacle in the sense of a mere ceremony.) The procession of palms is for us already a participation of the Pascha Domini. That is the blessing of this procession. It should therefore be, as far as possible, not simply a circular but a true linear procession, a genuine progress *from* somewhere *to* somewhere else, a procession whose destination differs from its starting point, insofar as the external circumstances permit. A grasp of this spiritual reality of the procession of palms will also provide the best means of intensifying the emotional reactions of the participants to a poignant empathy, an extraordinary sense of association with the salvific work of Christ.

The texts of this Sunday's Mass also portray the Pascha Domini in a way that must not be overlooked. The brief epistle has a most telling description of the passover of the Lord: "He ... humbled himself, becoming obedient to death, even to death on a cross. Therefore God also has exalted him and bestowed upon him a name that is above every name, so that ... every tongue should confess that the Lord Jesus Christ is in the glory of God the Father."

Precisely this text is especially illuminating for a proper understanding of the significance and importance of the expression *pascha*, passover. Modern devotional practice is largely accustomed to create a great gulf between the Passion and death of Jesus and his Resurrection. The first-generation apostolic preaching knew no such separation, would indeed have considered it to be meaningless, since the real redemption is not achieved simply by the death of Christ but only by the Resurrection. Thus, St. Paul does not say: If Christ had not suffered and died, the Christian preaching would have been groundless and absurd; rather he says, most definitely and emphatically: "if Christ has not risen, then our preaching is groundless, and your faith, too, is groundless" (1 Cor 15, 14). Certainly the Passion and death of Christ must not be effaced or obliterated, but neither should it be dissociated from the resurrection; and the beauty and grandeur of the word *pascha* lies precisely in its ability to interlace these two events. It dissociates neither the resurrection from the *Passion* nor yet the Passion from the *resurrection*. Both are the crucial points, initial and terminal respectively, of a single process, indeed a single event which is properly styled neither Passion nor resurrection but precisely pascha, passover, transition from one to the other.

In Introit and Tract, the congregation accomplishes this Passover of the Lord together with him. The worshipers pray many verses of Psalm 21, called the Psalm of the Passion. One need only compare the initial verses of this Psalm, from which are taken the corresponding words of Jesus on the cross, with the final verses, which also form the final portion of the Tract. Whoever prays this psalm—be it Christ or the Mystical Body of Christ, at all events Head and Members united in the praying Church— begins with the plaintive cry: "O God, my God, look upon me! Why have you forsaken me?" and ends with the triumphant declaration: "You who fear the Lord praise him ... The coming generation shall be told of the Lord, and the heavens shall declare his righteousness. To a people yet unborn, creatures too of the Lord."

A congregation praying the Psalm in this way (including the Gradual verses) is accomplishing the Pascha Domini. Out of the misery, anguish and affliction of this present time, it is proceeding, passing over in sacrificial community with its Lord into the glory of the "coming generation," the new age, the Kingdom of God. In this expectation does the congregation endure together with the suffering Lord the abandonment and loneliness of the Passion (Offertory) and is made ready in the Communion to drink the cup, according to the will of the Father.

It is truly a glorious festival that we keep on Palm Sunday as we cross the threshold of Holy Week. And the grandeur of the Passover keeps recurring in the ferial Masses of this week. It should be noted how dominant is the constantly recurring motif of the triumph of the suffering Christ; the accent is predominantly on the *saving* Passion to the almost complete exclusion of the usual notion of the *bitter* Passion.

The passover of the Lord also dominates the rites of Holy Thursday: the institution of the Eucharist, the washing of the feet, the blessing of the holy oils, the reconciliation of the penitents, solemnly ushered back on this day into the congregation of Christian worshipers from which they were banished in sackcloth and ashes on Ash Wednesday. The fact that all these grace-filled rites are assigned to the very day on which the Passion of Christ begins, is an insistent reminder of the temper of the praying Church when she solemnizes the public representation of that Passion.

This emphasis on the glory to which the cross leads is maintained even in the rites of Good Friday. The prayers and readings which we hear on this day out of the mouth of the Ecclesia are entirely in harmony with the tone set by the rite of Palm Sunday. We must never forget that the rite designated as the veneration of the cross quite evidently symbolizes the homage of the people of God before their *Lord exalted upon the Cross.* "Christ is *reigning* from the Cross." And in the midst of the Good Friday ceremonies we encounter the splendid declaration, "We adore your cross, O Lord, and we praise and glorify your holy resurrection! [We do this even on Good Friday!] For behold, by that wood joy came into the whole world."

Perhaps now we can grasp the extent of the loss of Christian substance when we consider and evaluate the Passion of Christ in a way that gives no attention to that other inalienable aspect of this sublime event; the Church still persistently calls attention to this duality even in these days, when she speaks of the "Passover of our Lord." In his Passover, we depart in penance from the world of death and enter into the glory of his kingdom. I could imagine that, were we to abide consistently in the Passover of the Lord, even our everyday life would be rendered much more intensely Christian. We should try this once during Holy Week, in the house of God and in our own homes. Let us reflect that every prayer, every reception of a sacrament, every celebration of a Eucharist, every overcoming of a temptation, every personal sacrifice has meaning and reality only if it occurs in the Passover of the Lord.

CHAPTER 11

Holy Thursday

At the very outset in the Introit, we unequivocally proclaim
the glory of the cross and in the other Propers we follow Christ
from obedience in death to his exaltation over the whole world.
At the Offertory we again praise the might of the Lord, the
power exercised by his right hand; whoever entrusts himself to
that right hand shall not die but live, and shall declare the works
of the Lord. The readings give an account of the last supper
(epistle) and the washing of the feet (gospel), both of them events
in which is manifest the unbounded love of the Lord for his little
band of followers.

This love of the Lord is experienced in a special way this day
by the penitents, who on Ash Wednesday were robed in penitential garb, sprinkled with ashes and excluded from the community of worshipers. On this Thursday, they were solemnly re-
conducted into the full fellowship of the community of worshipers,
in which community they were now permitted to participate fully
in the Passion of Christ, throughout the entirety of the eucharistic
rite. This reconciliation of the penitents is recalled in the Collect,
while the words of the Introit and Offertory surely express the
sentiments that must have stirred the hearts of the penitents on
this day.

These sentiments are, of course, still appropriate for us today,
on this day when we celebrate the institution of the Eucharist,
through which we are again and again granted the forgiveness of

sins. An insert in the *Qui pridie* indicates that the rite in the upper room is made present for us; this insert, peculiar to Holy Thursday (*hoc est hodie*), is to be found only in the Missal. This *hodie*—"today"—renders intelligible the designation of Holy Thursday as *natalis calicis*, "birthday of the chalice."

Especially beautiful is the set of antiphons sung during the washing of the feet, most particularly the one which the rubrics say may never be omitted: "Where charity and love are, there is God." This antiphon ought to be sung at our Holy Thursday rites even if the washing of the feet ceremony be omitted. It would fill the evening Holy Thursday rite still more with the generous love, overflowing into action, which illumined the last hours before the Passion of Christ.

But it is the consecration of the holy oils which renders most evident the abundance of graces granted us this day. In amazingly plastic terms, the hymn and the other texts praise the spiritual power of the holy oils (the oil of the sick, the oil of catechumens and holy chrism), that power which they receive from being consecrated. The entire rite testifies the great extent to which Christ uses earthly elements for the salvation of man by the communication of the Holy Spirit.

It is indeed regrettable that in our days the solemn rite of the consecration of the holy oils has such little meaning for the faithful. The extensive implications of the consecration of the holy oils even in civic life in former days is witnessed by the oldest German book of laws, the *Sachsenspiegel*, in which Thursday of every week is listed among the days of the truce of God on the grounds that: "On Thursday is consecrated the Chrism with which we are signed in baptism. On Thursday our Lord God did take the last supper with his disciples and it was the beginning of our (New) Covenant..."

It may be objected that the entire group of these ceremonies have little to do with the beginning of the Passion of Christ in the garden of Gethsemane. There are indeed only a few adumbrations of this inception of the Passion. The reason is to be sought in the whole notion of the Passion and death of Christ which we have already noted to be the basis of the rites of the Church. The Church sees not so much the *historical past* but rather the *abiding fruit* of the Passion of Christ, the salvation which that Passion assured. And so she concentrates an abundance of graces in the rites of this day before beginning the celebration of the Passion of the Lord. The living reality of the sacraments of baptism and penance, she portrays in the love of the Lord shown in the washing of the feet; the deliverance from sin she presents in palpable form in the rite of the reconciliation of the penitents. The consecration of holy chrism points to confirmation and holy orders, the consecration of the oil of the sick to extreme unction. The fullness of baptismal grace is likewise indicated by the consecration of the oil of catechumens and holy chrism. And all of this is dominated by the celebration of the holy Eucharist as the abiding witness to the love and the life poured out into this world by the great work of the Lord. In these rites, the Passion of Christ is not a historical past event but a superabundant living present for the congregation of worshipers.

On Holy Thursday the union of bishop and diocese, of pastor and congregation, is also clearly attested by the fact that but one Mass is celebrated in each church. Unity is reestablished by the reception of the penitents back into the congregation of the faithful. Unity is betokened by the paternal and fraternal love in the washing of the feet. The unity of the bishop with his diocese is exhibited in his consecration of the holy oils for all the parishes of that diocese. These holy oils are a bond of union between the bishop and every child anointed with them in baptism, every sick person receiving extreme unction, every candidate whom the bishop confirms, every church, every chalice, every bell anointed with the consecrated oils.

This Thursday of the last supper is thus a day full of great and deep mysteries. It reveals the far-reaching love of the Lord who in these rites truly draws to himself all things and all men: the great and the humble, the sinner and the saint, the healthy and the sick, the living and the dying; yes and even bread and wine and oil, the holy place and the sacred vessels and appurtenances. It is in very truth a day worthy to herald the salvific Passion of our Lord, the mystery of his cross.

CHAPTER 12

Good Friday

The Church's designation for this day is *parasceve*, "vigil," a designation taken over by the gospel writers from the Old Testament. A vigil is a day on which a watch is held, preparations are made for a feast day. And it is most fitting, indeed, that the day of the Lord's death should be called a vigil, because it points beyond itself and on it we keep watch against the great feast of the resurrection. The whole lenten period is indeed one long watch for the resurrection. The liturgical rites are full of associations of the cross with the glory of the new life; they have in them nothing of that somber mood of weeping and wailing which so often dominates sermon and devotions on Good Friday—unjustifiably as the following considerations will show.

With its lessons and responsories, then its solemn intercessions, the Church's worship service on this day preserves the very ancient form of Christian public worship. Anyone who is really attentive as he listens to the reading of the first lesson or reads it for himself will see clearly that it orients the community of Christian worshipers at the very outset of the Good Friday rites to the vocation to resurrection; and the same first responsory that speaks of the wrath of God also affirms that "his majesty fills the heavens, and the earth is filled with his praise." This note at the very beginning of the Church's official Good Friday rite must be emphasized again and again!

The same tone dominates the second lesson. For the preparations for the slaying of the paschal lamb are nothing other than the proclamation of the deliverance from the land of Egypt and the safe conduct back into the freedom of the messianic kingdom. The second responsory does indeed speak of the affliction of the man assaulted by the wickedness of the world, of the chosen people and of the "Servant of the Lord" in his sufferings; but even these verses end with the declaration: "Surely the just shall praise your name, and the upright shall dwell in your presence."

There now follows the Passion of Christ according to St. John. A right reading of this gospel account will likewise reveal the glory and majesty of the Lord in his Passion (as in the scene before Pilate and in the serenity with which he consummates upon the cross his life of service and of suffering).

The solemn intercessions are not only used on Good Friday; they represent the form of intercession used at every liturgy in Christian antiquity.

It is the unveiling and veneration of the cross which reveals to us the innermost meaning of the entire Good Friday liturgy. This begins with the threefold summons, "Behold the wood of the cross, on which hung the savior of the world! Come let us adore!" The covered cross is gradually unveiled and at the end, when it is elevated entirely uncovered, the entire congregation kneels to venerate it. This ceremony represents a public homage, celebrating the triumph of the cross. Nor is any discordant note introduced by what are called the *reproaches*. The oft-repeated antiphonal cry, "O my people, what have I done to you; wherein have I afflicted you? Answer me!" is not a lamentation but an *accusation* leveled by the Lord exalted upon the cross against his faithless people. And the congregation answers them not with expressions of sympathy but rather with the repeated cry: "O holy God! O holy strong One, O holy immortal One, have mercy upon us!"

Nowhere in the Church's liturgy is this fact so well expressed as here in the veneration of the cross on Good Friday: the cross is a royal throne and judgment seat, albeit the judgment is a judgment of mercy and grace. Anyone doubting this should consider the poignant antiphon sung during the veneration of the cross: "We adore your cross, O Lord, and we praise and glorify your holy resurrection ... by that wood joy came into the whole world." The triumphant mood of this text is underscored by the Gregorian melody which is the same as that of the *Te Deum!* And, as if this were not enough, this magnificent antiphon which sees cross and resurrection as organically linked is followed by another exultant hymn to the cross: "Praise, my tongue, the savior's glory. Tell his triumph far and wide; tell aloud the famous story of his body crucified; how upon the cross a victim vanquishing in death, he died." And all of this—we must emphasize the point again and again—in the somber darkness and sorrow of Good Friday! The Church is evidently celebrating this day from an entirely different point of view than the one we usually ascribe to her. Who must be reeducated, the Church or we ourselves?

Each individual member of the people of Christ performs the act of homage to his Lord exalted upon the cross by kissing that cross. This kiss is at once a sign of joyous union with the Lord triumphant in his Passion and a token of thankful homage for the sovereign love he has shown for us in that Passion.

The essential fruit of the Good Friday rites for every congregation is that each member shall learn to affirm in faith the triumph of the cross in the liturgical rite and then be able to celebrate that triumph personally by his conduct and posture in public as well as private life.

CHAPTER 13

Easter

THE PASSOVER OF OUR LORD

The name "Easter" with its uncertain and probably pagan etymology is most inadequate for the oldest and most solemn feast of Christianity, the "Feast of Feasts." It does not help us in the least to a better understanding of our celebration of this feast as Christians. The Church does, indeed, with her official designation *Dominica Resurrectionis*, point to the *event* we are celebrating: Christ is risen and has appeared to his own, apostles, disciples and pious women. But the Church uses this designation only for the one day, called the first day of the Feast. The subsequent days, even the following Sundays and the whole period of the Easter season, have no special title referring to the resurrection. They are called simply days and weeks *post pascha*.

Pascha is not a name for a specific event, the resurrection that distinguishes this day; rather it presents an *interpretation* of this event which initiates us into its meaning which girdles time and eternity and enables us to feel its power to link earth and heaven. Whereas *resurrection* still leaves some possibility of contenting ourselves with the recollection of the historical happening, the designation *pascha* bursts the bounds of any historical limitations. Pascha is the one great motif and therefore the ever-present theme of the divine plan of salvation. This is why the Church is so fond of this word and repeats it again and again in her readings, prayers and antiphons. We are therefore not justified in rendering this great word with the simple flat "Easter" which has nothing whatever to do with our festal rite or event. The Romance languages have retained something of the proper coloring in their designations, all derived from and recognizably related to the original *pascha*.

What, then, is pascha? It is a Jewish word meaning "passover," "transition," "passing over," and it acquired its salvation-history meaning in that night in which the angel of God smiting the first-born among the Egyptians "passed over" the houses of the Israelites, since these houses had been smeared with the blood of the paschal lamb, the "passover lamb." To these far-off events does that phrase refer that we hear so often in the liturgy of this season: "Christ, our Passover, has been sacrificed!" He is our paschal lamb, because he is the reason for death's passing us by. And so we are in an abiding passover, for death still passes the faithful by who have been washed and marked with the blood of the Lamb.

But the word pascha was to acquire still another, ampler meaning. Later it came to designate that great crossing of Israel out of Egypt, the land of death and the house of bondage, into the promised land, the holy land that was promised and given to the people of Israel as a kind of divine guarantee of the superabundance of life in the Kingdom of the Messiah. That was a splendid, a wonderful pascha, this forty-year pilgrimage from Egypt through the wilderness to Canaan: not always easy, full of afflictions and temptations, but for all that a glorious passage from poverty and misery to possession and abundance, from slavery to freedom, from death to life. But even this is but a symbol, most impressive and thrilling for anyone who penetrates to the depths of its meaning, but still only a prefiguration of what we celebrate in celebrating the Passover of our Lord Jesus Christ.

His passover is from the cross through death into the glory and majesty at the right hand of the Father, from Good Friday to the solemn rite of the Easter Vigil. That is the greatest and most triumphant passover that can be imagined. But this is not all. If we see the *death and resurrection* of Christ as the passover, then we shall realize that these two events are but two aspects of one great happening and that they can only be separated one from another on pain of losing the true sense of that all-embracing happening. What happened in that night when the angel passed over the houses of the Israelites, what happened when Israel was delivered out of Egypt and entered the promised land—all this finds its consummation in the culminating reality of the passover of our Lord. His passover involves his transition from lowliness to glory, from a life that was transitory and wretched into a new life that shall know no end and in which his human nature can no longer suffer and die. Such, in brief, is the passover of our Lord. It unites Good Friday so intimately with Easter that neither of these two days can be imagined without the other. Therefore does the glory of the resurrection shine forth in the Church's Good Friday liturgy; and for the same reason death is not dissembled in the Easter liturgy but rather portrayed again and again as the shore from which the pilgrim must cast off in order to cross to another land.

The first mood of the paschal season is the silence of the Holy Saturday watch; it is an aliturgical day. The Lord is resting in the tomb in which his body is not falling prey to dissolution as do all other bodies in the tomb but rather is being prepared for the glory of the resurrection. This glory begins to dawn in that truly blessed night which alone was granted the favor of knowing the day and hour of the resurrection. The Church portrays for us in many ways the passover of the Lord in this vigil rite: the new light struck from the dark and somber stone betokens with its bright flame the radiance of the risen Lord which spreads over the community of worshipers in the multitude of candles carried in procession into the dark church, where the congregation, assembled round the paschal candle, sings an exultant hymn of praise to Christ as the everlasting light.

An inspection of the ensuing readings from the Old Testament will show that here too the motif of the passover dominates in the salvation-history events. It culminates in the rites at the baptismal font and the renewal of the baptismal promises. For baptism is truly in a most crucial fashion the sacrament of the passover, inasmuch as we are removed by it from the kingdom of darkness and brought into the kingdom of light. The superb Preface for the blessing of the baptismal water presents this truth in a wealth of detail for our meditation and teaches us to understand the great mystery of our own baptism. We recall what was said to us in Quadragesima about the catechumens. They are now in fact experiencing the passover from death to life in baptism. Together with the catechumens and the penitents, each and every one of us has entered into the deliverance from guilt, into the passover of our Lord.

If the very brief epistle from the Letter to the Colossians is properly read and really communicated to catechumens and the entire congregation, the effect produced is surely unrivaled in poignancy in the entire liturgy of the Church: "... you have risen with Christ ... You have died, and your life is hidden with Christ in God. When Christ, your life, shall appear, then you too will appear with him in glory." It is here proclaimed to us on the authority of the apostle that the mighty passover of our Lord has indeed become also our own passover and that this identification will recur again and again until that moment at which it ends for us upon that throne on which the humanity of Christ is glorified at the right hand of the Father.

Whoever penetrates in faith into this message, infinitely transcending anything that the mind of man could conceive, will take up with a full heart the ever-recurring victory shout of the Alleluia and with it celebrate the triumph being solemnized by the community of Christ together with its risen Lord.

This victory is also the theme of the texts of the Easter Sunday Mass, especially the Sequence, which portrays the resurrection as the victorious issue of the conflict between death and life, from which our Lord emerges as victor and king.

When we have become familiar with this train of thought, we

shall find it easy to understand the incomparably beautiful Mass texts that accompany us throughout Easter Week. Again and again they present to us the two great twin mysteries of baptism and the Eucharist which so characteristically remind us during the time of our earthly pilgrimage of the passover of our Lord, in which we cast off in death that life, those possessions, that power that were perishable and transitory and win through to imperishable, immeasurable abundance in the Passover of Christ.

For this must be the abiding effect of our paschal rites: All of us together, as members of his Mystical Body, have been marshalled into the triumphant procession of the passover of our Lord Jesus Christ. His passover is the way of the Christian life.

"SONS OF THE RESURRECTION"

Our paschal liturgy begins in a nocturnal hour, in the glow of the new fire, in the radiance of the light that leads us to the "light-bearer" who brings up the new day, the new day that "knows no evening," to him who has "come back from limbo and shed his serene light upon mankind." We celebrate the night "which alone was found worthy to know the time and the hour at which Christ arose from the dead" and which therefore shines as brightly as the day: *Lumen Christi! Deo gratias!*

We must recognize the remarkable symbolism of this light with the "inward eye . . . enlightened" (Eph 1, 18) by the Spirit. Then we shall realize how everything prefigured in the Old Testament events has been fulfilled for us in the great Passover of our Lord. The hymn of praise to the paschal candle and the Preface for the blessing of the baptismal water point this up in extensive detail.

The Midnight Mass, at which in the primitive Church the catechumens used to receive the body of the Lord together with the entire congregation immediately after their baptism, is a very graphic demonstration of the way in which the passover of Christ becomes the passover of his people in baptism and in the participation in the sacrifice of Christ: passover from the perishable and transitory life of this world to the life that is immortal and unending, passover from this earth to the new dispensation. It is typical, indeed, of the entire paschal rite of the Church that in it the resurrection of the Lord does not remain insulated within itself but radiates the field of its spiritual force over the entire community of worshipers.

Thus, the epistle of the Midnight Mass acquires a very concrete meaning: "If you have risen with Christ, [and you have!] seek the things that are above, where Christ is seated at the right hand of God...you have died, and your life is hidden with Christ in God. When Christ, your life, shall appear, then you too will appear with him in glory."

These phrases of St. Paul develop the passover notion in its boldest form; their steep ascending curve describes the path of our own ascent in this solemn rite: and it is but natural that the sequel to this epistle should be the first crescendo of paschal jubilation in its most magnificent form.

In cathedral and abbey churches it is still customary for the deacon to approach the bishop or abbot after the epistle and solemnly pronounce the following words, "Most venerable father, I announce to you a great joy: it is the moment of the Alleluia." Thereupon the Alleluia is intoned and repeated by the entire congregation. Three times in succession there rings out in this fashion the primitive Christian victory shout, directly and quite concretely motivated by the resurrection of our Lord.

A special word on the "resurrection" of the Alleluia, its "homecoming." The word *alleluia* (praise God) is, to be sure, a very common and current word in all our liturgies; but precisely for this reason it is often simply rattled off thoughtlessly and unmelodiously with no proper appreciation of what is being said or why. A congregation which has learned to dialogue the Alleluia with its pastor in meaningful fashion could be said to have understood its own paschal, passover status.

For a proper understanding of the Alleluia, chapter 19 of the Apocalypse (vv. 1–8) should surely be consulted. It narrates the splendid scene in which the victory of God and the Lamb over all hostile powers is being applauded and acclaimed. From every corner of creation arises the Alleluia-shout, steadily swelling in volume and intensity, caught up and repeated again and again by countless choirs, by the four and twenty elders, representatives of the redeemed world, and by the four living beings, representatives of all the cosmic powers, to culminate as an exultant clamor "of countless multitudes—like the noise of water in flood, or the noise of deep thunder, as they cried out: Alleluia, the Lord our God, the Almighty, has claimed his kingdom!" That is the mystical sense of the message, *Christ is risen!*—an anticipation of the triumph of the Lamb!

No one who stops short at the mere historical event can comprehend the full significance of the mystery of the resurrection. I know of no passage in the New Testament which portrays the mystery of our paschal rite (always provided that rite is properly celebrated by the entire congregation) so eloquently as this scene from the Apocalypse, whose cadence is dictated by the fivefold Alleluia. For anyone who has grasped this affinity, the Alleluia dialogue and the frequent repetition of the Alleluia in the paschal season will be a joyous opportunity to realize his *own* victory and his *own* triumph with Christ.

The other texts of the Mass on the feast day itself maintain, in contrast to the strong current of emotion emanating from the multiplication of Alleluias in Paschaltide, a remarkable restraint which we feel especially strongly in the Introit. The text is a freely blended mosaic of various verses of Psalm 138. The somewhat obscure phrase, "I . . . am still with you" refers in the context of the Psalm to the incapacity of human minds to measure the lofty thoughts of the omniscient God. The psalmist means that his own creaturely mind would never entirely fathom the dealings of God and even if the creature should succeed in fathoming them, this would mean an absorption into the infinity of God. The Introit converts this text into a statement that can be put into the mouth of the risen Christ. His hitherto humbled human nature has found, in the glory of the resurrection, its supreme new dignity in the fullness of the divine life. But this same statement could equally well be put into the mouth of the just baptized catechumens and thus made to describe our own status as well. We have, in the passover, entered into the resurrection of the Lord, and after death has been vanquished in that resurrection our continuing existence is taken up into the endlessness of God. The living faith that accepts this will impart to the Alleluias inserted into the text of the Introit their proper harmony; nothing else will suffice!

The tendency to encompass the community of worshipers in the resurrection of Christ comes out clearly likewise in the other texts of the Masses of Easter Sunday and the octave. It is not for nothing that St. Paul speaks in the epistle of Christ as "our Passover," a phrase which we recapitulate at once in the Alleluia verse following the epistle and whose recurrence in the Communion verse ought to impel us to make of our communion at this Mass a total participation in the divinely ordained community with the passover of our Lord.

The gospel also, with its account of the women going to the tomb and the angel appearing in the empty tomb, gives clear indication of the way in which the resurrection of the Lord affects the first Christians. The women receive the commission to "tell his disciples and Peter that he goes before you into Galilee; there you shall see him ..." It is a fact which should not be overlooked that the Lord appears first not to the disciples but to the women and that these women are the heralds to the disciples of the message of the resurrection. The highlighting of the feminine element may be an allusion to the fact that even the disciples themselves are members of the great community of the bride of Christ and mother of the faithful, the Church, the community of Jesus Christ.

This same point emerges clearly on still another occasion, in the Sequence for Easter Sunday, in which the report brought by Mary Magdalene is immediately caught up and answered by the congregation of worshipers: "We know that Christ has burst the grave. Then, victor king, your people save. Amen. Alleluia!"

One recurrently and immediately palpable fact emerges from any proper external celebration of this Mass with thorough interior participation. In the Passover of Christ, we ourselves are accomplishing, as his community, his holy people, his Ecclesia, the passover from death to life. This is neither doctrinaire theory nor poetic fantasy; it is a reality surpassing all human experience, a reality substantiated for every mortal by the death and resurrection of Christ. We must clearly realize that it is only meaningful to sing, "Triumph now for death is vanquished," if we believe, in the face of all our natural experience, that there is no more death because even the dead resting in the grave are no longer under the power of death but rather have already within them the seed of the new life. This is the sense of the words of St. John Chrysostom from the Easter liturgy of the Byzantine Church: "Christ is risen from the dead, there are no more dead in the grave."

This, then, is the great insight to be drawn from the harmony of word and sacrament in the Paschal Mass: through the Passover of the Lord we have become "sons of the resurrection" (Lk 20, 36). As such, let us sing our Alleluia with ever increasing and deepening awareness and understanding in this joyous Paschaltide. In so doing, we are witnessing to his victory in this world and also in us, his Church.

CHAPTER 14

Low Sunday

The gospel shows us clearly how the resurrection of the Lord is communicated to his followers. He stands in the midst of his disciples, that is in the midst of the Church. He reveals himself to them as the risen Lord in a way that might almost be called sensory experiment: of his own accord, he shows to the eleven his hands and his side. But that is not the crucial point, this mere *seeing* him as the risen Saviour. He is aiming at something greater still, at communicating himself to us in a way hitherto quite impossible, in a way that transcends the senses entirely. As he has been sent by the Father, so does he send his followers. The mission he has received he communicates to them, as he fills them with his peace. His spirit, accessible to men only since his resurrection (Jn 7, 39) animates them and empowers them to vanquish and overcome death. For the remission of sins is objectively equivalent to the destruction of death whose very existence is "the wages of sin" (Rom 6, 23).

The graces and powers ascribed to the apostolic college in the gospel are thus in fact simply the resurrection of Christ operative in the apostles and therefore in the Christian community as well.

The dominant note of the epistle echoes this truth. The epistle opens with a fourfold mention of victory, of overcoming the world. This victory is promised to him who "is born of God," to his "faith" by which he believes "that Jesus is the Son of God." Such a man learns from the witness of the Spirit "that Christ is the truth." These phrases and indeed the entire epistle are seen in the light of the resurrection of Christ and its effect in and upon us; surely they must make us aware how great a mystery is this mystery of the Passover. For what does it mean to overcome the world? Certainly it does not mean to enslave the world, still less to smash the world brutally in pieces. To overcome the world means to cast off the transience of the world, the perishable element in it, in such a way that the mystery of God, especially the mystery of the incarnate Word and his resurrection become palpable and tangible. To overcome the world means to understand that he who was humiliated upon the cross has been exalted as lord over heaven and earth (Phil 2, 6 ff.), that everything in heaven and on earth is summed up in Christ (Eph 1, 10), that everything in heaven and on earth "subsists in him" (Col 1, 17). All of these are concrete assertions of revelation which make the cosmic character of the resurrection of Christ more clearly recognizable than does the vaguer phrase about victory over the world. In this context, the risen Lord appears not simply as "the truth," but rather as the ultimate reality in the Johannine sense.

This reality of the world in Christ and of Christ in the world is not so readily demonstrable in this present dispensation as is the fact of the resurrection attested by the wounds in the hands and side of Christ. It cannot be seen as Thomas saw those wounds. But only in this transcendent reality is there revealed the whole mystery of the resurrection of Christ in the full scope, embracing heaven and earth, man and the entire created universe. It is because this reality can only be grasped in faith that our Lord calls those blessed "who have not seen, and yet have believed."

It is of great significance that this word of the Lord to Thomas is expressly repeated to the newly baptized and to the entire congregation in the Communion verse; for we are all in danger of leaving the resurrection of Christ out of account in our picture of cosmic reality, whereas it is only in the light of the resurrection of Christ that the totality of existence can be comprehended in its trinity of the water and the blood and the Spirit. We recall that, as early as the Postcommunion of Easter Sunday itself, we prayed for the outpouring of the Spirit.

CHAPTER 15

Second Sunday after Easter

The oft-recurring passage in Scripture, "The earth is full of the mercy of the Lord. By the word of the Lord the heavens were made," is concretized by the fact of the resurrection of Christ, in which the Christian community participates. The incorporation of mankind into the resurrection of Christ is truly the crowning mercy of God. No matter how grievous the catastrophes that come upon mankind, whole peoples and individuals, the fact that we are risen in Christ (Eph 2, 6; Col 3, 14) is an irrefutable proof of God's mercy and love for each one of us. The confession of this fact is the necessary prerequisite for the Mass of this Sunday. Priest and people must unite in this confession.

St. Peter in the epistle announces to us the Passion of the Lord as proof of the mercy of God. "Christ . . . bore our sins in his body upon the tree, that we, having died to sin, might live to justice." This statement, too, must be referred to the paschal mystery and so made into a concrete declaration concerning the state of the congregation here assembled for worship. Living "to justice" is not to be understood simply in an ethical sense; "justice" in the Pauline sense is the perfection, the glory of God (cf. Rom 5). And so the concrete sense of this passage is as follows: You, the recipients of the letter and the community now met for worship, have been lifted out of the stream of the life of Adam which leads to death and are now in the stream of the life that flows from the risen Christ through all the generations of mankind and leads to the glorious life of God. A genuine and effective proclamation of this epistle requires that the reader do more than simply read out the words of St. Peter to the congregation as words long ago addressed to communities of Christians. Rather the reader must, as commissioned herald of the word of God, address the words directly to his audience in the church before him. The congregation must understand that the words "you were as sheep going astray" refer precisely to it, to this community of Christians here assembled.

If the congregation understands the dynamic of this Mass, then the final words of the epistle point naturally to the good shepherd, whom the congregation of worshipers here assembled "recognizes" now in the celebration of the Eucharist, even as the disciples once recognized him in the breaking of the bread. And if the worshipers have not yet grasped this point, then the Lord will himself announce it to them in the gospel: "I am the good shepherd. The good shepherd lays down his life for his sheep ... I know mine and mine know me, even as the Father knows me and I know the Father; and I lay down my life for my sheep."

The "good" shepherd is not merely the kindly shepherd. "Good" here implies rather the conscientious shepherd, who does everything a shepherd should do, who fulfills without reservations his pastoral office. And the shepherd is not only the one who feeds the sheep in green pastures; in the idiom of antiquity he is also the king who leads his people.

The question arises as to whether Christ has indeed done everything that pertains to the office of the conscientious shepherd. He did not deliver his people or his country from political and economic distress. And even today he allows misery and even undeserved affliction to persist; war, plague and natural calamities to continue to rage. In the face of these facts of experience it is an understandable question for men to ask if Christ could not better discharge his pastoral and regal office than in fact he is now doing. The answer is the same as that given in the epistle: he has laid down his life and by his death won for men life eternal, true immortality.

In this faith, the congregation will no longer feel any constraint in their attitude to the good shepherd; they will hail him and acclaim him, knowing that he recognizes each of them and they recognize him (in Communion). And so they enter into the power and glory of their good shepherd.

CHAPTER 16

Third Sunday after Easter

A dominant note in this Sunday's Mass is one that is to be found in the gospel accounts of the risen Christ. For Mark tells us that he appeared "in the form of a stranger" (Mk 16, 12), with the result that he was not recognized by the disciples on the road to Emmaus, nor by Mary Magdalene, nor yet by the disciples on the lake of Galilee. He was in fact a stranger to them inasmuch as he had already entered, by the extinction of the life of Adam, by his resurrection, into the new dispensation and had laid aside "the forms of this world." This is attested to by the fact that he no longer appears for a protracted period in this dispensation. Always it is but "a little while"; his abiding habitation is "with the Father" from the very moment of the resurrection.

But the consequence of this is that those whom he has incorporated into his resurrection no longer belong to this world. Rather they are "strangers and pilgrims" in this world. Again it should be noted that the pastor must address his congregation with these words of St. Paul. He must, in the context of the accounts of the resurrection of Christ, put to himself and his congregation the earnest question: are they really prepared to draw the straightforward conclusion from their co-resurrection with Christ, namely that they are henceforward only "strangers and pilgrims" in this world? Should the congregation not believe him, the pastor need not have recourse to lengthy expatiations of his own; he can and should rather let Christ speak to them with that unique force and conviction that his words always carry: "Amen, amen, I say to you, that you shall weep and lament, but the world shall rejoice; and you shall be sorrowful ... but I will see you again ... and your joy no one shall take from you." These words of Christ need no lengthy explanation: either a man believes them and feels himself bound by them, or he does not believe them and simply ignores them. But in the latter event, there can be no true celebration for that man of the passover of our Lord.

Once again, any congregation meaningfully initiated into intelligent participation in the Mass should know these things already from its understanding of the resurrection mystery. For when the congregation prays in the Alleluia verse: "Thus Christ should suffer and should rise again from the dead and should enter into his glory," it is describing with these words its own destiny, precisely because it has died and risen again with Christ. A properly educated congregation will therefore not be at all disturbed or puzzled by Christ's predictions of the afflictions awaiting them; on the contrary, all the texts of this Mass which are assigned to the congregation express the unbounded joy and jubilation felt by the community of worshipers at their entry, together with their Lord, into the presence of the Father.

Certainly if we are aware of the "little while" of our lives on this earth and nonetheless are full of jubilation, we may participate in the splendid serenity of the risen Lord.

CHAPTER 17

Fourth Sunday after Easter

If the texts in Introit, Alleluia verse and Offertory, "Sing to the Lord a new song...shout joyfully to God, all the earth," be taken only as a sign of an all-pervading joy in God, they lose their actuality for the congregation and can easily become empty phrases. They must rather be interpreted in the light of the message of the resurrection. Then they acquire their concrete topical significance for this Sunday's Mass, as do the other passages: "His right hand has won him victory...the right hand of the Lord has lifted me up.... The right hand of the Lord has exercised power...great things the Lord has done for me." The words of the liturgy must be used to drive home to the faithful the fact that something of immense import has happened to them through their participation in the resurrection of Christ. They must be brought to admit with their *Cantate* and *Jubilate* that this is the crucial reality of their life and all the other texts must be made the expression of the new spiritual reality of the worshiping congregation.

This is also the insistent note of the epistle for it, too, must be understood in the light of the passover. The priest should expressly declare that these are not his own words but rather those of God's revelation. It is God himself who stands before the community of worshipers as "the Father of Lights." These lights are the celestial luminaries which radiate light and warmth. They are signs of his life-giving munificence, but he is not subject to alteration as are the constellations. His radiance shines upon us without shadow of alteration, for we have been begotten by him through the message of the gospel, the word of truth, and are therefore truly sons of God. The nexus with the resurrection of Christ is established. These passages of revealed scripture must not be simply "quoted"; they must be "proclaimed." This means that the congregation of worshipers is to be told in the words and with the authority of God exactly what it has become through the resurrection of Christ. Only when the congregation has grasped this in the light of faith will their *Cantate* and their *Jubilate* be really genuine; only then will they be able to testify before the whole world, "The right hand of the Lord has lifted me up. Come and hear: I shall tell you the great things the Lord has done for me."

This should be the homiletic intention. That such an exaltation and such a victory is possible is guaranteed to us by the words of Christ in the gospel concerning the advocate he will send us. This is he who will testify to the world of the victory of Christ. The Spirit is the one who will glorify the Lord in his Church. The intimacy of the association of the Christian community to the triumph of Christ through the instrumentality of the Spirit is shown in the Communion verse which repeats the words of the Lord from the gospel. It is with unquestioning trust in this promise that the Christian community this Sunday enters into union with its Lord in the Eucharist. This text, which links the paschal mystery with the day of Pentecost, achieves the declaration—beyond the power of the unaided human tongue—of the secret that we are made by this rite "partakers of the one supreme divinity."

Who would presume to make such a declaration if he did not speak in the power of the promised Spirit? The priest must embolden the congregation to hazard this declaration, strengthened by the supernatural virtues of faith and hope. If the congregation does this, then it has grasped the innermost meaning of this Sunday's Mass.

CHAPTER 18

Fifth Sunday after Easter

Of the doxologies in Introit, Offertory and Communion verse in this Sunday's Mass, the same thing must be said as was said last Sunday. They must again be interpreted in the light of the resurrection of Christ and the Christian congregation; for "Christ has risen and has given light to us, whom he redeemed with his blood" (Alleluia verse). Again and again the congregation must be shown in this Paschaltide that it is really the community of the risen Lord, a community which not only hears with joy the exultant cry, *Resurrexit* but proceeds to proclaim it "to the ends of the earth." For "he is risen" is synonomous with "the Lord has delivered his people" (Introit).

The persistent proclamation of this message is of supreme importance for a proper spiritual exploitation of the paschal season; for it is only by such persistence that the congregation can be trained in an authentic attitude of mind—and this should surely be the motivating aim of all conscientious pastoral endeavor.

Such an understanding of the interrelation of these texts clearly indicates where the emphasis must be placed in the readings. For what is said—and this means *revealed*—in the readings forms the basis for the specifically Christian attitude of mind.

"The Lord has delivered his people" says the Introit, and the epistle accordingly shows us the way to a thorough understanding of "the perfect law of liberty" so that we can make it operative in our daily life. Law and liberty usually appear in the context of the Kantian autonomy and heteronomy as mutually exclusive concepts. But in the sphere of Christian existence there is in fact "the perfect law of liberty." The Christian community must be familiarized with this. The will of God is indeed for man an extraneous will, because it is precisely an expression of the *divine* life and not of *our* life. But after we have become "partakers of the one supreme divinity" through the resurrection of Christ (Secret, fourth Sunday after Easter), this very law of the life of God becomes an expression and the native mold of our own being elevated in God. We have truly entered into the "freedom of the children of God," albeit only to the extent to which we admit with faith and love that our existence in Christ, the risen Lord, is the consummation of our humanity. That this is no mere empty theorizing is shown by the astonishing words of Christ in the gospel. These words are to be instilled into the congregation as precisely the words of Christ himself: "In that day you shall ask in my name; and I do not say that I will ask the Father for you, for the Father himself loves you because you have loved me, and have believed..." The faculty, accorded us by our union with the risen Christ, of praying in the name of Jesus results in our prayer being treated by the Father as the prayer of his own only-begotten Son. This is surely the supreme proof of the freedom we have attained in the Son of God. And this is and will always be the abiding fruit of the resurrection of our Lord Christ. It is the intrinsic intent of this Sunday's Mass to drive this truth home to the congregation, and this should form the full and exclusive motivation of this Sunday's preaching: the Father loves us because we love the Son and believe in him.

CHAPTER 19

Ascension Day

In his ascension, the Lord withdraws from his disciples and from all mortal men his humanly perceptible physical presence. This was a necessary consequence of his resurrection. For, although his risen body was and is indeed still dust of the dust of this world, that body has been elevated into an entirely new mode of existence, we might say into an entirely new conformation which no longer fits into the forms of this world.

Thus St. Peter can proclaim, "He [Christ] must have his dwelling-place in heaven until the time when all is restored anew" (Acts 3, 21). This same notion of a teleologically oriented interval occurs in the epistle as well and has been assimilated from there into the Introit: "This Jesus who has been taken up from you into heaven, shall come *in the same way* as you have seen him going up to heaven." A like significance is ascribed by the Church to the ascension in the proper Preface and *Communicantes* of this Mass: "[Christ] was taken up to heaven ... so that he might make us sharers in his own divinity" and "... celebrating the most sacred day on which your only-begotten Son our Lord placed at the right hand of your glory the frail nature of ours which he had taken on himself."

These texts make evident the salvation-history significance of the ascension of Christ, that is, its significance for the Christian community of worshipers here assembled. Jesus continues to belong to his flock on earth and his flock continues to belong to him, for the "frail nature of ours" is exalted in him and placed at the right hand of the Father. The ascension of the Lord has thus in no sense attenuated, still less dissolved, our union with him. But the ascension, clearly highlighting as it does the refashioning of our humanity, does lead to a certain *tension* between Christ and his flock on earth. This tension he will himself terminate when he comes again. The deepest reason for his second coming is to take home the world and mankind into his new phenotype and mode of being resulting from the resurrection. The tension will thus persist until "the time when all is restored anew," or until the hope of the whole of created nature "to share in the glorious freedom of God's sons" (Rom 8, 21) is fulfilled.

The ascension must therefore be so presented as to make palpable both elements: the exalted Lord and his flock on earth are united, yet they are separated by the distinction of the mode of existence. He has already assumed for his own humanity the form of the new dispensation and is thus become a stranger to this old world in which we still find ourselves. Thus the ascension of the Lord becomes the triumph of the Lord over the world and all that is in that world. The verses taken from Psalms 46 and 47 in Introit, Alleluia verse, Offertory, and Communion verse, all bear witness to this triumph. Both Psalms celebrate the triumphal entry of God into his sanctuary, into his city. By singing these texts, the congregation is associating itself to this triumphal procession.

But—and this is the other aspect of the ascension—his triumphal entry is possible only to those who free themselves from the forms of this world. In the forms of this world the glory of the risen Christ cannot be abidingly enjoyed. And so the ascension of the Lord becomes a signal and unmistakable witness on the part of Christ and the Church to the transitoriness and insufficiency of the forms of this world. The congregation is struck by the fact that the risen Lord and his flock are strange to this world, but this sense of alienation is not a cause of pain or sorrow; rather it is swallowed up by the triumphal entry into the imperishable glory of the new dispensation. And so the ascension as a feast forces us to decide whether we are prepared to enter with Christ into his glory at the right hand of the Father, even at the price of a very drastic, and if need be total, detachment from the forms and fashions of this world which have become so familiar and dear to us.

The entire problematic contained for the Christian community in the diligent and conscientious celebration of the feast of the ascension could be dramatically portrayed by asking at the outset why we do not wish one another *Happy Ascension* when an analogous greeting is so unthinkingly taken for granted as suitable to the other great Christian feasts! Many people these days would take it as a joke if they were wished a *Happy Ascension*. Yet in reality such a greeting would demonstrate our preparedness for the celebration of this great feast.

CHAPTER 20

Sunday after the Ascension

This Sunday's Mass confirms the Christian community in the "ascension" posture and frame of mind. In the Introit Christ's "little flock" is already expressing its longing for its exalted Lord, seeking after his countenance with heart-felt desire, begging him not to hide his face from his own for he is their light and their salvation. In Alleluia verse and Offertory, the congregation again exultantly acclaims the triumph of its Lord and meditates on his promise: "I will not leave you orphans; I go away, but I will come to you, and your heart shall rejoice." The apostle Peter admonishes the Christian community in the reading to be prudent and watchful in prayer to this Lord and to make the gifts and graces of their Lord accessible to all in mutual charity and love. It is the vocation of this flock of Christ to see to it that "in all things God may be honored through Jesus Christ, our Lord." It is for this that Christ has called and gathered his own and left them in the world, and the ascended Christ does not take his followers out of the world but rather leaves them in it (Communion verse) so that they may be witnesses to him. The gospel passage is a concrete application of the admonitions of the epistle. Christ's words make it abundantly clear what bitter and grievous consequences can ensue from the fact that his followers have been taken up together with him to a new mode of existence. "They will expel you from the synagogues . . . everyone who kills you [will] think that he is offering worship to God." Is such a promise still gospel, still *glad tidings*? Certainly not of itself! But it is assuredly *glad tidings* for the faithful inasmuch as the endurance of affliction is a witness to Christ's victory over the world and consequently a sign of our own victory over the world.

The congregation must be most emphatically faced with this consequence of participation in the ascension of the Lord. Christians must learn in this eucharistic rite to decide if they are prepared to understand and to endure all manner of persecution in the train of their ascended Lord. Each and every one of them, priests included, must learn to make this decision. What is at stake is whether the words of Jesus, "Blessed are they who suffer persecution for the cause of right; the kingdom of heaven is theirs" are simply an inconsequential pious phrase or whether they express the divinely revealed explanation of what it means to be a Christian in the world. Whoever preaches to the people on this Sunday must put to himself and his congregation the question: Do we celebrate the ascension with tears in our eyes or with a victorious Alleluia, if we really believe in these words of our Lord? Above all, the grace of God should be invoked in this Mass, to the end that an honest answer be given to this question by priest and people, and that it be the right answer. How can we do this better than in the words of the Postcommunion, "Grant, O Lord, that we may always abide in *thanksgiving*."

CHAPTER 21

Pentecost Sunday

There are many members of our congregations who, although they do know that pentecost is the "feast of the Holy Spirit," can make nothing of the word pentecost itself. It will therefore be a good idea to explain to them that pentecost comes from the Greek word *pentecostes* and means "fifty." The ordinal numeral is of importance because it links the feast of pentecost with Easter; this nexus might otherwise too easily be lost sight of. Pentecost is not an independent feast of the Holy Spirit but rather the feast of Christ on which the world-wide effect of this redemption begins to unfold. This feast celebrates the ingress into history of the triumphant power of Christ. Of this the Lord himself spoke again and again in his farewell addresses (cf. the gospels of the last few Sundays).

The sending of the Spirit by the Father in the name of Jesus (Jn 14, 26) is in fact the *crown of his redemptive work.* The sending of the Spirit by the Father in the name of Jesus, that is in most intimate ontological union with him, gives rise to the new mode of union beween the Lord exalted at the right hand of the Father and his disciples, and consequently with redeemed humanity in the Church and likewise with the whole of creation.

The promise of Our Lord to the disciples in today's gospel, "...the Advocate, the Holy Spirit...will...bring to your mind whatever I have said to you," does not mean simply that the Spirit will recall it to their minds, but rather that he will make it their interior possession. The disciples will truly "become party to" what Jesus has said, and the result will be that the Lord himself will no longer be simply *among* them as he had been in the past, in the days of his physical presence, but will rather be *in* them, by the power of his Spirit poured out upon the disciples in his name by the Father.

This outpouring is recounted to us in the Acts of the Apostles. This account clearly shows that the outpouring of the Spirit was not simply a communication to the apostles of special graces of office. The entire company of the hundred and twenty mentioned in Acts 1, 15 receives the Spirit who "came to rest on each of them" in what seemed to be tongues of fire. This is not properly brought out in the pictorial representations of the event nor unfortunately in the modern text of the Pentecost *Communicantes* in the Roman Missal which makes the quite unwarranted statement that "the Holy Spirit appeared to the apostles [!] in the form of countless tongues." This formulation is a regrettable contraction of the primitive *Communicantes* which can be found in the most ancient Sacramentaries: *Communicantes et diem sacratissimum pentecostes celebrantes, quo Spiritus Sanctus apostolos plebemque credentium praesentia suae majestatis implevit.* This primitive formulation, with its all-embracing statement that "the Holy Spirit filled the holy apostles and the company of the faithful with the pervading presence of his majesty," clearly indicates the real pentecostal event: the Spirit fills the hundred and twenty with his majestic pervading presence and the Christian community becomes the *phenotype of Christ,* his body. Filled with the Holy Spirit, the Church becomes not the (mystical) body of the Holy Spirit but by the Spirit is made the (mystical) *body of Christ.* The first action of the Spirit-filled company is not the convert sermon of St. Peter; that begins only in verse 14, after the end of the passage we read today. The first action of the Spirit-filled community is the speaking "in foreign tongues, even as the Holy Spirit prompted them to speak." This is ecstatic jubilee entirely within the confines of the company of the faithful. The essential point here seems to me to be this: that first

Christian community is actually experiencing in the Spirit what it means to be Christ's Church. We *believe* this with all that it involves, but this community *experienced* it, experienced the be-atifying mystery of the Church, which the community of Christians could not express in their own local human idiom, which they uttered in strange exultant tongues molded by the Spirit.

But it is not only the Christian community which is filled with the Spirit. In the Introit, the community of worshipers proclaims, "The Spirit of the Lord has filled the whole world, and that which contains all things has knowledge of his voice." This signi-fies that the exalted ascended Lord is penetrating, with the out-pouring of his Spirit, the whole world and taking it up into the new glory of his transfigured body, albeit for the moment in secret and latent fashion.

We must mediate to the congregation in the Mass of Pentecost a living and vital sense of this all-embracing, cosmic power of the Spirit sent by the Father in the name of Christ. The venerable phrase from the Psalm in the Alleluia verse, "Send forth your Spirit and they shall be created and you shall renew the face of the earth," must be rendered vitally intelligible to the congrega-tion in its towering historical and cosmic significance. Only then will the oft-repeated clamor for the Spirit, *emitte Spiritum, veni Sancte Spiritus,* become the expression of a genuine interior craving.

This frame of mind also makes us confident that the Lord will, in this our act of sacrificial worship, "make lasting what you have wrought in us, O God," that operation begun in Jerusalem, the molding of the Christian community by the instrumentality of the Spirit into the body of Christ. And so our Communion will be full of exultation, and of us it will be able to be said, as once it was of those first disciples, that "they were all filled with the Holy Spirit and began speaking of the wondrous deeds of God."

This should be the grace for which we pray in our Pentecost Mass and which we strive after in the fashioning of the rite and the proclamation of the word.

CHAPTER 22

Trinity Sunday

I doubt that the dogma of the blessed Trinity means much in the daily lives of many of our parishioners. In any event, the most important concern of any sermon on Trinity Sunday should be to make the nexus of the blessed Trinity with this congregation now before us so vital that the community of worshipers will really be roused to a grateful and exultant affirmation of the pulsing cycle of life and love within the triune God and consequently be rendered capable of divining the infinite perfection we attain as "sons of God in the one Son of God" by our participation in the interior life of the blessed Trinity."

The texts of this Mass make this insistent demand upon us in most concentrated fashion. Almost all of them express but one single thought and this, in the main, in almost identical words: "Blessed be the holy Trinity" (Introit); "Blessed are you, O Lord, who behold the depths," "Blessed are you, O Lord, in the firmament," "Blessed are you, O Lord the God of our fathers" (Gradual); "Blessed be God . . ." (Offertory); "We bless the God of heaven" (Communion verse).

What can we do to prevent this six-fold doxology from evaporating into a spiritual insipidity? We cannot simply ignore it. The first thing we must attempt is to mediate to our listening congregation a hint of the splendor and indescribable power of the vital currents that pulse reciprocally among Father and Son and Spirit. We must try to make so vivid to the congregation that act in which the Father thinks and expresses in one Word, the *Logos*, the whole of the infinite abundance of the divine life, that the Christians who hear us will begin to divine what creative power inheres in this cognitive act. Then we should present an equally graphic portrayal of the process in which the Father and the Son communicate their love reciprocally in the Spirit, so that our hearers will be genuinely thrilled by the love, surpassing all human capacity and ecstasy, that is the very life of God. Perhaps the phrase of the fathers will help us here: they called the Holy Spirit "the kiss of the blessed Trinity."

Somehow our words must convey the tremendous truth that in God thinking and loving do not remain mere abstract thought or simple feeling but rather that in each of these operations the whole of God's infinite fullness is personalized. Of course, many in the congregation will not entirely understand all this but many —perhaps more than the preacher often thinks!—in every congregation will be startled into attention at the thought that we can penetrate so deeply into the interior life of God, because he has granted us this insight in his revelation. Even if they do not fully grasp all the theological implications, they will at least arrive at the conviction of the immensity and blessedness of the interior life of God and of the great gulf that separates him from us in whom all thinking and loving is radically unfulfilled and therefore never entirely satisfying.

Those who reject a *personal* God are not always atheists; often they do so simply because they are unable to imagine God within those cramped confines that we all experience in our own personal existence here on earth. God is precisely entirely other, entirely different from us: this is the general insight that we experience nowhere else so poignantly as in the contemplation of his triune being. So enormous is his vitality that it is not exhausted in a single personal existence but rather nourishes the divine fullness simultaneously in three Persons, all of whom remain nonetheless united in the one Godhead. The problem of "individual and community" which weighs so heavily upon us is here resolved in a way that surpasses all human conception. And this is a faint hint of the perfection of God.

In view of the total ignorance of many Christians concerning the interior life of God, it will be not only desirable but necessary to preach on Trinity Sunday about God and his interior life. It is a recurrent complaint of many churchgoers that they hear comparatively little in sermons about God himself!

The second point of departure in any treatment of the texts of this Mass is provided by the circumstance that the praise of the Trinity is three times expressly motivated (in Introit, Offertory, and Communion verse) by the fact that "he has shown mercy to us." We should make clear to our hearers that God's mercy to us must not be understood merely generically in this Sunday's Mass. Rather this Mass points up a special aspect of that mercy: it is by his mercy that we are permitted to know and love him in the ultimate intimacy of his life as his revelation displays that life to us, and that he not only permits us to gaze upon the mighty currents of his knowing and his loving, but even takes us up, in an incalculable elevation and exaltation, into this interior life of his. This is borne out by the gospel, according to which we are baptized in the name of the three divine Persons and therefore enter into an intimate union with them in the supernatural "divine" virtues of faith, hope and love. The epistle also, whose first level of meaning has to do with the mysterious ways of God to man (Jew and gentile alike), shows us precisely in this context how the interior secret of the divine life sustains and perfects us.

If we speak thus about the triune God, the congregation may really, by the grace of God, sing the six-fold praise of the trinity with heartfelt gratitude and exultant joy, in accord with the acclamation in the *Gloria in excelsis*, "We give you thanks for your great glory."

CHAPTER 23

Second Sunday after Pentecost

All the texts we use today at this Mass of the second Sunday after Pentecost can be traced back to ancient sacramentaries and antiphonaries from about the year 800. They must be interpreted in the light of the great salvific actions of God culminating in the sending of the Spirit, a culmination which was also a spatial and temporal initiation of the historical unfolding of these salvific actions in the Church as the people of God. Otherwise there is a great danger that sermons on the Sundays after Pentecost will simply bowdlerize these texts, an offense which would be specially regrettable precisely in the case of these texts!

This becomes clear as early as the Introit of today's Mass: "The Lord came to my protection, and he led me out into freedom; he saved me, because he loves me." These are graphic statements and their vividness must be preserved in the sermon we preach about them; they must be applied to what has happened to this (let it be stressed: *this*) community of Christians, *this* congregation as a result of the incarnation, the Passion of Christ, his resurrection and the sending of the Spirit.

Equally concrete should be the questions posed by the preacher to his congregation: How have you been "led out into freedom"? Have you then really been *saved*? What signs do you see to indicate that God loves you? How is Christian living a living in freedom? Why is it that being a Christian is synonomous with being free? Such questions must be insistently posed to the congregation. Not in the style of the old tub-thumping oratory, not in a manner that tries to convince by shouting and roaring, but rather in a simple, quiet fashion which does not stampede the congregation but rather leaves them time to assimilate the questions and really think them through. We find an answer in the epistle: "We know that we have passed from death to life." Question: do our congregations these days still know that God has allowed them to take this great step, the step into his freedom? Are they aware that the reason the world hates them is that they have passed from death to life? The epistle expresses the fact of God's love for us as follows: "In this we have come to know his love, that he laid down his life for us." Is it still true of us in these days that the death of Christ and his resurrection provide an irrefutable proof of his love even if everything else in our life is going wrong?

The congregation is well aware of the hate of the world, hence the fervent appeals to God in the Gradual. But the congregation is also aware of the God who lives and operates in its midst, hence the Alleluia and the succeeding verse.

And the great banquet in the gospel parable surely reveals in this context a wider range than its usual restricted eucharistic application. Is not everything that God has wrought for our salvation an invitation to his banquet, that is to blessed union with him? Is not the statement that God has invited us to a delightful and nourishing banquet a fine gloss on the words *freedom* and *salvation?* Away from our everyday world with its streets and houses, away to the banquet! And it should here be noted that the commitments mentioned by the parable as standing in the way of the invitation to the banquet are very grave and important matters. In order to preserve the graphic note, the question should perhaps be raised as to whether the men mentioned in the parable were not indeed justified in giving preference to the grave obligations of their state in life and consideration for their bride over the invitation to a banquet. For we have here quite clearly a contrast between the so-called serious business of living and the pleasurable conviviality of a banquet.

The sense of the parable is therefore that it is a *pleasure* to be a Christian, a sentiment that is surely echoed in the *celestis vita* (heavenly life) of the Secret. And is not such an interior posture and frame of mind the necessary prerequisite for a completely honest and genuine rendering in prayer or song of the Communion verse, "I will sing to the Lord, who has given me all good," as applied to the participation granted the congregation in the great banquet of the Eucharist? It is with such sentiments of pleasure and delight that the congregation ought to leave this Mass if in it they have decided, against all the seriousness of the world, in favor of the joy and beatitude of salvation as prepared for them by God in Christ. What a fine goal to set for this Sunday's sermon that it should lead the congregation to this decision, or better still inspire them to be confederates in it.

CHAPTER 24

Third Sunday after Pentecost

Despite the power of God's operation in his Church, despite the multiplicity of sublime gifts and powers he has entrusted to her, the praying Church remains aware, even in the accomplishment of her most exalted rite, of her human frailty and sinfulness. And precisely on these Sundays after Pentecost, she repeatedly proclaims the paradoxical juxtaposition of *already* and *not yet*. *Already* we are redeemed but *not yet* perfected; *already* we dwell in the power and glory of the divine sonship through Christ, but the assaults of the world and Satan are *not yet* ended; *not yet* has the human wretchedness been put off in the phenotype of the Church as a whole and in her individual members, although we may *already* pride ourselves hopefully in the coming glory.

And so the words of the Introit of today's Mass must be said with candor and honesty as a statement about ourselves, about the whole Church, hierarchy and laity alike: "... I am alone and desolate ... my poverty and my pain ... pardon all my sins." All false self-confidence, all boasting about powers once granted is swept aside by the imploring cry, "Look upon me, O Lord, and have pity on me!" and it is unreservedly avowed that without God "nothing is strong, nothing is holy" in the Church, that it is God alone who so leads and guides us that "we may so pass through things temporal that we lose not the things eternal" (Collect). It does the entire Church good to reflect in all seriousness upon this radical state of the ecclesiastical community. I believe that priests need to make this meditation as well, so that they should be able honestly and with conviction to confess to the congregation *mea maxima culpa* and to say with equally honest sincerity and conviction the *nobis quoque peccatoribus* in the Canon which, as the cognate *famulis tuis* clearly shows, is intended in the first instance to refer to priests. This mediation would perhaps make it easier for them to find the proper tone in admonishing or even scolding the congregation.

The epistle likewise initially highlights the *not yet*: whatever affliction, misery or anxiety may come upon us we have but one course of action, to "humble" ourselves "under the mighty hand of God"; the tempter is still hard at work and we must resist him. That is the *not yet*. But the *already* is also proclaimed. We are a chosen band, for "the God of all grace ... has called us unto his eternal glory in Christ Jesus," and this vocation is the foundation *already* laid for the certain hope that he will "perfect, strengthen and establish us." Therefore do we exultantly proclaim, even in the *not yet* state: "To him is the glory and the dominion forever and ever. Amen."

The trusting acceptance of these words of God's revelation concerning the hidden but truly present glory of God impels the congregation to speak words of encouragement to itself in its loneliness and misery: "Cast your care upon the Lord and he will support you ... God is a just judge, strong and patient. Shall he be angry all the time?"

That God is really so disposed is shown by Jesus' parable of the lost sheep and the lost coin. Sometimes the interpretation of this parable lays too much stress upon the redemption of the individual. It should be borne in mind that there were 100 sheep and 10 coins, numbers which indicate an integral totality. Ninety-nine and nine are not simply one hundred or ten minus one; they indicate the destruction of the integral totality. Example: a deck of cards or a set of chessmen becomes entirely useless and valueless if but one card or one piece be missing. If a chain of ten coins constituted the dowry of the Jewish woman, then the chain was rendered valueless, because of the destruction of its integrity, even if but one coin were missing. And so these parables have to do with the integrity of the work of redemption. The Fathers on several occasions point out that the Logos left the angels and the heavenly hosts in order to seek and find and bring home again the human race lost on earth; and that the joy in heaven is the joy over the restoration of the integral totality of the elect by the return of redeemed mankind, which is the Church. Thus the sheep found again and the coin found again is the Church and the heavenly rejoicing is for the Church which stands in contrast to the just "who have no need of repentance."

Because the congregation is in this attitude of penitence, it gleans from the words of the gospel the confidence that in the sacrifice of Christ it will find a gracious God (Offertory). The words of this Offertory and the thoughts behind them grow out of the texts of the the Mass of the word: awareness of human frailty and infirmity mixed with firmest trust in the mercy of God. The congregation which enters thus into the sacrifice of Christ and experiences in that sacrifice, despite all the *not yet* involved in the human lot, the fact of the participation in the life of Christ, is the congregation to which is addressed the word of Christ, *dico vobis*, in the Communion verse. And so the dynamic of this Mass is complete: what began as the cry, "Look upon me, O Lord," ends with this answering assurance from that Lord that there is joy among the angels over this congregation.

CHAPTER 25

Fourth Sunday after Pentecost

The praying Church is remarkably steadfast and persistent in confessing, in the Masses of the Sundays after Pentecost, the dual heritage promised by the Lord in his farewell addresses (cf. the gospels from the third Sunday after Easter to Pentecost Sunday, including the Masses of the vigils of Ascension and Pentecost): the assaults, temptations and *hate of the world*, and the merciful and gladdening *love of God*, who unites himself with his flock through his spirit in Christ. And so the "ferial season" after Pentecost sets for the community of Christian worshipers the task of efficient administration of this dual inheritance. Christians must not only endure the assaults and temptations of the world but must triumphantly overcome them in trusting reliance upon the power of the living God.

The fourth Sunday after Pentecost is a classical example of this. The very first sentence of the Introit indicates the tension in which the Church finds herself. There are enemies all around who are fearsome in themselves, but there is also God who is "my light" and "the protector of my life." And so the atmosphere around the congregation of worshipers clears into the serenity of the exclamation "Though an army shall encamp against me, my heart shall not fear." This is the state of Christ's flock! This is our state! And everything becomes much more concrete still when we consider that *illuminatio* was in antiquity the technical term for baptism, that the newly baptized were simply designated as *illuminati,* and that the *life* whose *pro-tector* is the Lord is that life that we have received in baptism as risen with Christ. *Light* and *life* have in very truth been the Spirit. I consider the constant reference back to Easter and Pentecost on these Sundays to be not only objectively in accord with the texts but also essential in order for the Christian community of worshipers in our day to grasp their position in the salvation history dynamic.

How seriously the worshiping congregation takes the tension of its situation, despite all interior riches and all inner glory, is shown by the Collect and especially by the Gradual. The picture of the pilgrim Church is dramatically evoked by the words of the Collect, praying God to "let peace guide the course of world events, that your Church may serve you in peace and security," while the Gradual is a challenge to us to remember our own sinfulness and its destructive consequences—*us,* the priests as well as the congregation.

We must certainly do more during the celebration of the Mass than simply present these texts to the community in our official capacity, for we are an integral unity with that community and must therefore speak these texts as a personal declaration, just as much as does the ordinary member of the congregation; we must be aware of the fact that the texts apply to us. Many of the laity are rightly annoyed at the fact that not infrequently the speech and gestures of the priest at the altar give the impression that the entire rite is simply a formal ritual without personal significance for priest or congregation. Nor can this unfortunate impression be glossed over by external ceremony or even pious stereotypes in the celebrant's movements and gestures. We have here to do with imponderables which, in order to be effective, require not so much that the priest protract the text of the Mass by lengthy meditative pauses (the meditation should have been done before the Mass) but rather that he so pronounce and articulate it that everyone, including himself, can grasp its sense and inner significance.

This holds also for the readings. How comforting is the statement in today's epistle that, although "the sufferings of the present time" do indeed afflict us, they "are not worthy to be compared with the glory to come that will be revealed in us." How comforting it is for each of us in our personal pastoral activity to learn from revelation that even that world which so often estranges us from God and therefore seems lost, that all that vast expanse of created nature other than man "will be delivered from its slavery to corruption into the freedom of the glory of the sons of God." For this means that our world and we, the Christian community, are called to the glory of God.

It is against this same background that we must understand today's gospel. This gospel is certainly in no case intended to portray the blessing accruing to Christian labor when performed in the name of Christ. There is something quite different involved. Peter does not rub his hands with joy at the miraculous catch of fishes, the result of his work in the name of Christ. Rather he prostrates himself before the Lord and is smitten by an awareness of his own sinfulness! He does not deign even to cast a second glance at the fine catch of fish. He does not even express his thanks for that catch to the Master who has evidently revealed something to Peter that drives all other thoughts and concerns out of the fisherman's mind. There are but two poles of reality: Peter the sinner and the mysterious Master; and the latter is the crucial reality. So Peter does not return with renewed energy to his business (as the Master's blessing upon his labors would, humanly speaking, give him every reason to do); rather Peter and his partners bring their boats in to land, leave them simply standing there and follow Jesus. This, then, was the result of the miraculous catch of fish: the abandonment of earthly business in order to follow Christ. Palpably evident is the disparity between the glory of Christ in the work of his disciples and therefore also in his Church and the things of this world (cf. beginning of epistle). Peter and his partners who respond to the call of the Lord thus become the antithesis of those invited guests who declined the Lord's invitation to the banquet with their weighty middle-class excuses (cf. second Sunday after Pentecost).

May our eyes be opened even as were Peter's so that this Mass may show us where true reality, true life is to be found for us and the world! Therefore do we pray in the Offertory, "Give light to my eyes that I may never sleep in death," and in the Secret that God may, in this our sacrifice in Christ, "by the constraint of your mercy, make even our rebellious wills submit to you," a prayer that combines humility and generosity in a poignant expression of our true state, in our human misery as Church of Jesus Christ. And then when we receive him in Communion we shall, like Peter, recognize him in his mysterious transcendency, as our support, our refuge, our deliverer and our helper (Communion).

What a glorious expanse is opened up before us by today's Mass! Any priest who ingresses into it humbly together with his congregation will here become what Paul, with all due respect for his apostolic authority, wanted to become: "Not that we would domineer over your faith; rather, we would help you to achieve happiness" (2 Cor 1, 24).

CHAPTER 26

Fifth Sunday after Pentecost

The Introit of this Mass obviously continues the line of the Introit of last Sunday, a sign that in the season of Pentecost that same spiritual continuity is maintained which is the foundation of any genuine instruction and education, as opposed to the modern methods with their constant preoccupation with novelty in order to sustain "interest." This sort of interest leads in the best event to a superficial knowledge of many things but it never results in any genuine, vital molding and education of the whole man.

There is something further of great importance to say about this Introit. If its sentiments, recited or sung during the entry, are a genuine expression of the frame of mind and interior attitude with which priest and congregation are coming before the altar, from above which in antiquity the picture of the Pantocrator dominated the church and consequently the congregation, then they acquire the character of a trusting *homage* to that Lord to whose worship the congregation is now about to address itself. The Kyrie and the Gloria will then unfold perfectly organically out of this Introit so understood and rightly performed, and the statements of the Introit will communicate to both Kyrie and Gloria a new accent which will rescue them from the formalism into which they unfortunately often lapse, as is witnessed by the tone and speed of their recitation. Introit, Kyrie and Gloria ought, in this Mass, to become in very truth an impressive *like-minded* (epistle) act of homage on the part of the worshiping community of Christians before the majesty of their Lord and God.

Continuing this homage, the Collect begins with a solemn recognition of the "joys beyond understanding" which this Lord and God has prepared for "those who love" him. With these joys in mind, the Collect proceeds to implore that passionate, all-surpassing love which can merit the promises of God "which are far superior to anything we can desire."

In order that we have a proper conception of this love, we must consider that the love of God is never simply a superficial kindly or friendly feeling, but is rather the love that "has been poured out in our hearts by the Holy Spirit, whom we have received" (Rom 5, 5). It will therefore be desirable to remind the congregation that we are a congregation *after Pentecost*, consequently a congregation in the Holy Spirit.

It is in this light, too, that St. Peter's admonitions in the epistle acquire their properly Christian significance, those admonitions to like-mindedness in prayer, mercy and compassion, love of enemies which answers cursing with blessing. The crucial ground of all these demands and exhortations is that we ourselves, as the flock of Christ, have been "called" to "inherit a blessing" (if the congregation does not know and believe this, then the purely human reaction will be to answer curse with curse). This also makes plain what is meant by the promises of God mentioned in the Collect. The certainty of the reality of such a blessing does away with that fear that so often overcomes us human beings; for as flock of Christ we have nothing to fear, insofar as we "hallow the Lord Christ in [our] hearts." These words, too, from the very end of the epistle must be addressed directly to the listening congregation and, in order to prevent this phrase from evaporating into mere formalism, something should also be said about *how* a person hallows the Lord Christ in his heart. In any event, this phrase presupposes an ontological *Christ in us* (outpouring of the Spirit: members of the body of Christ!) and requires of us that we give this sovereign presence room in our thoughts, words, and works, of which the admonitions uttered by St. Peter in this epistle are exemplary. And this attention to Christ's ontological presence within each one of us causes the fulfillment of these admonitions and requirements to transcend its merely ethical significance. And certainly the congregation which stands this Sunday in homage before the altar and whose faith is strong ought to be ready to fulfill all these admonitions and requirements as a simple component of its homage. And this is why the congregation confirms this readiness in the Gradual and the Alleluia verse which contain new phrases of homage which on the one hand serve as a continuation of the Introit and on the other hand constitute the answer, the response to the last verses of the epistle.

But such homage must not remain merely superficial. Against any such tendency the gospel warns that external actions are not enough, the crucial thing is the foundation, the love which binds the congregation into a like-minded unity and links it inseparably to Christ. This love, for which the Collect had already prayed, molds the congregation anew into a spiritual unity in the offertory action. But where today are the oblations of the individuals to be found? Where are those gifts that are offered to be distributed when consecrated, the many loaves that become the one loaf and represent the unity of the congregation, a consideration to which Pius XII, following Benedict XIV, has called the attention of priests with cogent emphasis? In today's Mass, the Secret is an evident resumption of the last admonition of the gospel; but it also indicates how the unity comes out in the sacramental sign: "May the gift of each individual . . . aid the salvation of all men."

CHAPTER 27

Sixth Sunday after Pentecost

The same thing must be said about the Introit of this Mass and its nexus with Kyrie, Gloria, and Collect, as was said about last Sunday's. And this opportunity should be taken to point out quite expressly to the congregation that we appear today in an identical attitude and frame of mind for the identical public business before the altar of the Lord, in order to become more proficient at it and make it our own interior possession. The words change but the spiritual bias remains the same; much appears in a more urgent and insistent formulation. The congregation confesses itself to be God's people and his inheritance; so dependent upon him is this community of worshipers that, if he heed them not, they "become like those who go down into the pit."

A word would here be in place concerning the forms of address we use to God in the Collects, sometimes adjectival, sometimes relative clauses expressing particular attributes of his being and operation. These forms of address are often themselves theological propositions. Today's Collect offers especially fine formulations which are not simply theoretical propositions but are extensively and very graphically, even plastically, illustrated in epistle and gospel. For baptism and the Eucharist are the foundation laid by Christ himself for the life, the communal life, of the Christian community; precisely herein does God reveal himself as the "mighty God, author of every good thing." This should be strongly emphasized. The entry into the divinely ordained community with

Christ through dying and rising again in the sacrament of baptism, the being nourished by Christ in the Eucharist—all of this is a reality in every Christian congregation and becomes a reality again today in the celebration of the Eucharist. The nexus with pascha comes more clearly into focus: every Sunday is a paschal feast! We acquire participation in the passover of Christ through the mediation of the love of God in the Holy Spirit, the Spirit of Pentecost.

The application of the gospel to the congregation assembled for the celebration of the sacrificial rite is confirmed in the Offertory: "Keep my steps steadfast in your paths, that my feet may not falter ... Show your wondrous kindness, for you are the Savior of those who trust in you, O Lord." The echo of the word of Christ in the gospel ("I have compassion on the crowd ... they will faint on the way") and the reference to the gospel-reported miracle ("wondrous kindness") are unmistakable.

All of these considerations render intelligible the exultant joy of the Communion: We, the community of Christian worshipers, are pilgrims who live on what they receive from the house and the table of the Lord, so that they may not faint on the way.

CHAPTER 28

Seventh Sunday after Pentecost

On this Sunday the homage of the congregation of worshipers to its Lord and God acquires a new nuance. The congregation boasts in joyous pride of its sovereign lord and of his power over all rulers and peoples. The Christian community must learn this, nothing should be stronger or more vivid in its mind than this one truth: "the Lord is the Most High, the awe-inspiring; he is the great king over all the earth." This Introit should serve as foundation for Kyrie and Gloria. As on previous Sundays, it penetrates into the Collect, expressing joy at the power of God "whose ever-watchful providence rules all things." This power of God is the basis of the humble trust expressed in this prayer.

The estimate and performance of the service rendered a master depends on the opinion held of that master and of his power. The notion of the service of God must be grasped more clearly against this background. The epistle points the way: various sorts of service, slavery and wages are here contrasted. The service of uncleanness in the sacrifices to idols and demons entails slavery to sin, and sin's payment for services rendered is death. The service of justice, as accomplished in union with the sacrifice of Christ in the Christian life of self-sacrificing service, may indeed make us seem to be "slaves of God," but this "slavery" is different from the former sort. The slave of God receives not the *wage* appropriate to his paltry and beggarly service but rather the *gift of grace* from God, which is "life everlasting in Christ Jesus our

Lord." This Sunday the Christian community must again elect, on the basis of this proclamation, the service of the Lord, the *opus Dei*. The Gradual, directly following the epistle, admonishes Christians to such a choice. It is essential that *this* congregation understand the dignity and the glory of that service it is now offering to God in the eucharistic sacrifice. Only then will the Alleluia verse come from the heart of the congregation; only then can the community of worshipers really triumph in the service of its priestly king.

Substantially the same message is contained in the gospel. Christ points the way to a triumphal entry into the kingdom of heaven. Necessary prerequisites are, on the one hand, that we recognize the false prophets as precisely that and refuse to follow them (for following the false prophets would parallel the slavery of uncleanness in the epistle) and, on the other hand, that we do not content ourselves with empty words but rather do the will of the Father (or as the epistle puts it, be slaves of justice and therefore of God). The interior bond between epistle and gospel becomes evident in the repeated reference to fruit to be borne: fruits of the slavery of uncleanness and fruits of holiness in the epistle, good and bad fruit in the gospel; but in both cases the fruits connected with service to the evil or the good.

The service of God is accomplished preeminently in sacrifice, at least now in this rite! And so the Offertory typifies by the Old Testament sacrifice of the chosen people the mystical service rendered by the congregation in the sacrifice of Christ. But the contrast between service and service again becomes palpable in the Secret where sacrifice and sacrifice are contrasted: the many offerings of the Old Law and the one perfect sacrifice. This perfect sacrifice is the sacrifice of the Catholic community of worshipers in the Eucharist. In a passage paralleling that used on the fifth Sunday after Pentecost, it is said of this sacrifice that "the individual gift, which each of us presents in honor of your name, may bring all of us closer to salvation."

This service of sacrifice is our redemption; in it and through it God unfolds his *medicinalis operatio* which frees us from evil inclinations and leads us to do good. And so the Church shows a candid awareness of our tendency to be attracted more by the *evil* than by the *good* (Postcommunion). She knows that those who have believed in the Lord still incline to run after false prophets. She realizes that the company initiated by baptism into the service of Christ often flirts with the service of another! She knows all this, but she does not therefore simply admonish or scold like a shoddy pulpiteer; rather she causes us to admit our own weakness and implore God's grace in prayer. May God forbid that this Postcommunion should ever be a mere vacuous "Lord, Lord."

CHAPTER 29

Eighth Sunday after Pentecost

In the Introit the congregation of worshipers gratefully praises the mercy and loving-kindness of God, who reveals his glory and power in the magnitude of his mercies. A magnificent beginning for a Christian worship service! But the life of many in the congregation during the past week may well have been hard, pitiless, and without apparent mercy. Will they nonetheless be able honestly to proclaim, "We have received your mercy, O God," despite sickness in the family or lack of success in work? What sort of a *mercy* (kindness) is it which the people of Christ are here praising? The epistle provides the answer: "Now you have not received the spirit of bondage . . . but you have received a spirit of adoption as sons, by virtue of which we cry, 'Abba! Father!' The Spirit himself gives testimony to our spirit that we are sons of God. But if we are sons, we are heirs also: heirs indeed of God and joint heirs with Christ."

This, therefore, is the mercy of God which we received "in your temple" when we were baptized. Will that mercy be extinguished or rendered illusory or muffled by the unmerciful pace of everyday life? In this matter, the Christian must decide in the community of God, in the company of God's faithful servants. On his decision depends his capacity truly to assist at this Mass, to assist in such a way that he can sing at the end together with the people of Christ (no matter what has happened to him during the week): "Taste and see how good is the Lord; blessed is the man who trusts in him." (Communion)

Not content with stating what we have received, the epistle also indicates that from which we have been delivered: we are no longer debtors to the flesh. This is to be taken quite concretely and realistically: we owe nothing to the flesh for we have already abandoned everything that we received from the flesh through being born according to the flesh. All this we have relinquished in our dying together with Christ in order to receive from him the *new* life, through which we are henceforth "debtors" to the Spirit (sixth Sunday after Pentecost). The things of this world, of this dispensation, have therefore no immediate worth for us any longer; they have become "alien" to us as St. Jerome puts it in his homily on the gospel of this Sunday. And so we are in the situation of the unjust steward of whom the gospel parable tells. It would, however, be better to call this parable the parable of the "prudent steward" for Christ's purpose in telling this story is to hold up the prudent wisdom of the steward, not his injustice, as a model for us. We are summoned to forge a path for ourselves into everlasting habitations, using the mammon of wickedness with which we can achieve substantially nothing for our Christian existence, inasmuch as it is alien to us as Christians. But by using it, we as "children of the light" make more profit on our earthly capital than "the children of this world"; the only prerequisite is that we survey and cope with *our own* situation with the same discreet and wary prudence with which the children of this world survey and cope with theirs. Now the secret of our situation is this: "children of the light" that we are, we are "debtors not to the flesh" (epistle), since we "have received . . . kindness, O God, within your temple" (Introit) which has made us "heirs indeed of God and joint heirs with Christ." The disconcerting assaults we suffer from the flesh make clear the fact that our debt to the flesh has not yet been paid in full, that we are presently in possession of the "first-fruits of the spirit" but not as yet of his visible fullness. And so the supplications in Gradual and Offertory are fully justified in our situation; but what carries the day is the realization of "how good is the Lord"

(Communion). This is the fruit of sacrifice and sacrament, perhaps also a fulfillment of our sincere and openhearted petition in the Collect for God to grant us "always the spirit to think and act rightly." The petitions in the Secret show the same dispositions as we pray God to "sanctify our lives on earth and bring us to eternal happiness" (gospel: "everlasting dwellings").

We profess in practice our awareness of the fact that we are debtors not to the flesh but to the spirit by our conscientiousness in the accomplishment of this sacrificial rite for the performance of which we have had to withdraw from the world in some way, involving a greater or lesser exhibition of sacrifices and prudence. Is it not, for instance, genuine prudence for someone to use his free time not simply for a pleasant weekend or a round of Sunday sport but rather for the service of the Lord? Therein lies the *reparatio mentis et corporis* which we implore in the Postcommunion as the fruit of "this heavenly sacrament." We desire it to "repair" us, to "put us in order," to restore us to our rightful mind—we who were perhaps inclined during the week to envision the world as our creditor by un-Christian conceptions of business or social life (recall the guests invited to the banquet). We desire that restoration of the proper equilibrium in "soul and body" so that we may take our proper place one day not only in the hidden sacramental event of the Eucharist but also in the fully matured reality of the divine inheritance, in eternal happiness, in the everlasting dwellings.

CHAPTER 30

Ninth Sunday after Pentecost

The two Scripture readings in today's Mass will be a good starting point from which to guide the congregation to the proper interior and external rendering of the other texts of this Mass. Both epistle and gospel in today's Mass portray for the communities of the New Testament people of God the jeopardy and the rejection of the Old Testament people of God. Like a solemn exorcism sounds the six-fold cry of the epistle: "Do not ... even as some of them. ... Neither let us ... as some of them." The same sins and lapses of which the old Israel was guilty can befall the Christian community as well, perhaps have already befallen one or another in that community or at least "some of them" even if not all. God's reason for having recorded in the Holy Book the various forms of defection from him and rebellion against him of which the history of Israel is full was certainly not simply to pillory his chosen people before history, so that we might look down upon it with scorn from the heights of our own proud self-assurance. Rather, all these things have been recorded "as a type ... for our correction," who in these latter days are exposed to the same peril "as they." If we are presently standing fast by and in the grace of God ("... eternal life as a free gift [grace], through Christ Jesus our Lord"—Rom 6, 23), we have no right to presume that we shall always so stand; rather we must reckon with the chronic possibility of a fall.

It is simply and solely the unfailing mercy of God upon which we may set our hope that temptation will not overcome us. God has not pledged himself to make it easy for us in the afflictions that assail us from without (political, economic, and social problems; natural calamities, sickness, misery, indigence, and death) and from within (temptations against faith, scandal in the Church, failure to obtain satisfaction in the matter of our demands, even our just demands). We have not been promised an easy time of it but we have been promised the strength and power of God to enable us to *endure* the severest trials; this notion of "endurance" presupposes precisely the severity of the trial (cf. Ap 6, 11; 11 1 ff.; 13, 10).

Christ's tears over Jerusalem are a confirmation at the dawning of the messianic age of the same fact instanced by St. Paul with examples from Israel's distant past. For the sins of that past of the chosen people culminated in Israel's rejection of her Messiah and refusal to receive his message. Jerusalem and Israel are dashed to the ground and given over to utter destruction because they did not recognize the moment at which God was visiting them in his Christ. (The word "visitation" in the gospel should be either paraphrased or explained since it is usually synonomous today in general usage with the infliction of penalties or the occasioning of suffering.)

But here again, this judgment upon Israel has been recorded solely for our sake. In exactly this manner will God punish any Christian community failing the genuine encounter with its Christ. Now when does a congregation fail such an encounter? I think in all cases where its life and action as a community of worshipers dissipates itself in *superficialities*, in mere externals, in pharisaic pedantry and scruples. The danger of such superficiality has been described with vivid clarity in the Apocalypse (2, 1 ff.; 11, 1–2). And so the eucharistizing congregation is faced with serious facts involving serious duties. Its proper response is indicated in the other proper texts of today's Mass. God alone is helper and savior in all such situations (Introit); this truth the congregation must realize and confess anew today. God's omnipotence ensures the spread of his glory and renown over all the earth and our own deliverance from the enemy (Gradual); this conviction must also be solidified today in the heart of the congregation, precisely in the face of the menace and threat which the readings so emphatically level against the congregation.

It is only such faith that teaches us that all the ordinances and judgments of God are not only "right" but "give joy to the heart" of God's people, regardless of their issue here on earth. From this realization (Offertory) there follows the unreserved devotion of the congregation to the sacrifice of its Lord, being accomplished in this Mass before this congregation and in it (Secret). This sacrifice and this sacrificial devotion culminates for the congregation in the communion of the body and blood of Christ. This communion assures the most imperilled congregation that the Lord abides in it and it in him (Communion). And this must suffice for the Church militant here on earth.

CHAPTER 31

Tenth Sunday after Pentecost

This Sunday's Scripture readings are just as much a mirror of the congregation as were last Sunday's, regardless of the difference between the Old and the New Covenant.

The enviable state of the Christian congregation is brought out in the epistle, which crystallizes the contrast with the heathen community and pagan worship, with its implications of ignorant and suggestible manipulation expressed in the phrase "you went to dumb idols according as you were led." Bisping notes in his Commentary (1855) that the Greek text is most emphatic in conveying this notion of "the power of the pull and the drive, and the well-nigh blind abulia of the pagan addicts." In Christian worship, on the other hand, the one *Spirit* of God holds manifold dominion. Of this Spirit, St. Paul writes: "Those who follow the leading of God's Spirit are all God's sons; the Spirit you have now received is not, as of old, a spirit of slavery, to govern you by fear; it is the spirit of adoption," (Rom 8, 14 f.) and "where the Lord's Spirit is, there is freedom" (2 Cor 3, 17).

The first effect of the operation of this Spirit is the confession, stemming from grace-mediated knowledge, that Jesus is Lord of all. The sentence "No one can say: 'Jesus is Lord'" (note that this is the sense, not simply "Jesus Lord"—we have to do with a judgment, not a mere invocation) cannot be taken lightly. It must be borne in mind that *kyrios* has a political significance, endowing the sentence with an absolute sense of unlimited confession of the kingship of Jesus. Paul may here have written "Jesus" instead of "Christ" with the deliberate intention of highlighting the historical personality of the Saviour (cf. Bisping, *op. cit.*). This kingship of Jesus the crucified who no longer thrones visibly upon earth is beyond the grasp of mere human knowledge. Even as Peter's confession (Mat 16, 17), it can only be formulated in the illumination of the Spirit in the teeth of that political, cultural and moral reality accessible to the unaided human mind: "Jesus—and no one else—is the Kyrios, the supreme Lord!"

Do our congregations these days formulate this confession with that same spiritual awareness and conviction? Does the *Kyrie eleison* which is assigned for the congregation to dialogue or sing still possess today in our Masses this tremendous sense of testimony? The first sentences of the epistle might well provide a good opportunity to direct the attention of the congregation emphatically to the fact that it is their duty to confess with these acclamations that Christ is Lord of the world.

Paul proceeds to unfold the whole wealth of the flock of Christ flowing from the freedom and power of the Spirit in the variety of gifts and offices. The picture should be rounded out by a comparison of the remaining verses of Chapter 12 following the pericope read at today's Mass. There is a real wealth discernible in the versatility of functions here described which makes our present-day rites and ceremonies seem almost beggarly and impoverished by comparison. I do not mean the luxuriance often displayed in liturgical ceremonies in the sumptuous and clamorous staging of incidentals, but rather that wealth of spiritual endowment of the congregation shown in the versatility of their *participation* in the worship of God.

Are there not a great many "churchgoers" in our parishes who fulfill their so-called Sunday duty only under the pressure of the precept of the Church and accordingly sit out (or stand out!) the Mass in a wooden-faced disinterest calculated to inhibit the most extroverted celebrant? The introductory sentences of this Sunday's epistle is much more topical than we priests think.

We must then as priests make every effort, really do everything in our power to render such incongruous behavior impossible. Pius XI says in the Apostolic Constitution *Divini cultus* of December 20, 1928: "It is truly most essential that the faithful do not . . . assist at the sacred rites as strangers or mute spectators (*extranei vel muti spectatores*)." We cannot and must not spare our congregations of laity and clerics this glance in the mirror of the epistle.

Equally topical is the distinction between the two types of congregation which comes out in Christ's parable in today's gospel. No one of us will dispute the fact that there are pharisees and publicans still today in the Christian community. Self-congratulation, casting of a balance sheet with God, are practices which have not yet died out and are unlikely ever to die out entirely. But it would be bad were the congregations in our Churches not constantly alerted to this danger of sanctimonious self-righteousness, and worse still were such self-righteousness encouraged by many pastoral practices, however well meant. The parable of our Lord shows us unmistakably where are the roots of Christian perfection and how it behaves before God.

Our look into these two mirrors ought to result in our returning home "justified" from this Mass, insofar as we have really conformed ourselves in self-forgetful humility to the service of God in the Mass and become aware of our human poverty and wretchedness vis-à-vis our Kyrios. The other Propers of this Mass again afford us assistance here: thus, we do not boast of our own will power and achievements, but rather cast all our care upon him (Introit); we place ourselves with childlike trust under his protection, knowing well that he alone is the arbiter of our fate (Gradual); we enter unreservedly into the sacrifice of our Lord, to whom we profess our homage and loyalty in Offertory and Communion verse.

Finally, we should help the congregation to grasp and retain the splendid and vitally practical theology animating the Collect; this would be a fine contribution to the topic of "the plastic theology of the liturgy." The almighty power of God is "made most evident in . . . mercy and pity." This picture of God shines forth for us from the Scripture readings which mirror the state of the congregation; and we acknowledge and profess this picture of God in the other proper texts of this Sunday's Mass.

CHAPTER 32

Eleventh Sunday after Pentecost

Every Sunday is, in its inspiration and origin, a celebration of the resurrection of Christ, even though this aspect does not receive explicit expression in every Mass text. And when a Sunday Mass contains direct reference to the resurrection of Christ, then the congregation should be insistently reminded each time of this crucial event, fundamental for the origin of the Church and for the lives of each and every Christian.

This Sunday's epistle might be termed a veritable catechism of the resurrection of Christ. It is the consummate quintessence of *the gospel* which had been handed down to Paul by the original disciples together with the fact of the apparitions of the risen Lord to individual disciples, to smaller and larger groups of disciples and even to "more than five hundred brethren at one time." Finally Paul himself became a witness of this glory of the risen Lord who met him on the road to Damascus. Thus Paul can with perfect justification hand on what had been handed down to him and what he had himself experienced as *gospel*. He has confirmed the Corinthians in that gospel, they have built their new way of life upon it and will be saved by it, if they but hold fast to it.

This is in fact a simple straightforward catechism on the fact of the resurrection of Christ. We ought not to scruple at presenting it on this Sunday in all its simplicity to our congregations, not of course merely in order to impart historical religious knowledge, but rather to show that it is upon the incorporation through faith into this event that our salvation depends, regardless of our past and present state or station. For us, even as for St. Paul, it is true that "by the grace of God, I am what I am." Once again the important thing is for the congregation to grasp two interrelated facts: first, that it really *is* something, to wit a community and therefore body of the risen Lord, and then, that it is this solely and exclusively by grace.

This is the basis for an understanding of the succeeding Gradual whose resurrection motif is unmistakable in the context (God helps me: my flesh thrives once again) and of the truly paschal exultation of the Alleluia verse. The Introit too should be explained in terms of this epistle picture: God causes us, his people, to dwell in unity in his sanctuary, in power and strength. A recognition of this truth will permeate the congregation here assembled within the four walls of this church building with the illuminating conviction that they are an image here on earth of the heavenly sanctuary and the throne room of God. This conviction should be specially strong in the congregation today as it harmonizes with the angelic choirs in the great Sanctus hymn. In this way, the congregation learns not simply from instruction but from the personal accomplishment of its mystery as Church of Jesus Christ; and this as a result of the powerful effect of the resurrection of Christ. Once again it is true of the congregation that "by the grace of God I am what I am."

The miracle of the healing of the deaf-mute, reported in the gospel, points to this new level of reality that is the resurrection. All the miracles of Christ, especially the miracles of healing, have, without prejudice to their historical reality, an eschatological bias, inasmuch as they point to the integrity of life which will be attained in the last days in the resurrection of the flesh. We all suffer, quite understandably, from the imperfection of our speaking and of our hearing here on earth. The deaf-mute in the Gospel, after his cure, "began to speak correctly," and the crowd was so impressed as to exult: "He has done all things well." We know better than that crowd of old just how the Lord will do all things well when he reveals, in the resurrection of the flesh, the glory of matter in man and in the new heaven and new earth. Then and then only will we be able to hear aright and to speak aright. For the third time, thus, we find confirmed St. Paul's statement in its application to the Christian community and congregation of worshipers, "by the grace of God I am what I am." For what we shall be on that great last day is even now planted as a seed within us, since God has already "given us the foretaste of his Spirit in our hearts" (2 Cor 1, 22; 5, 5; Eph 1, 14).

In the great joy of the Passover we therefore proceed to unite our sacrifice with that of our Lord who has healed us (Offertory), even as he healed the deaf-mute in the gospel. It is the Lord, too, who will fill our barns with abundance and make our presses to run over with wine (Communion verse). So will we experience the fullness of eternal life in our sacramental sacrifice on this earth, an answer to the prayer we prayed in the Collect, that God would "forgive us and grant us the blessings we dare not presume to ask for." This formulation is very illuminating for a theology of prayer.

All of this should conspire to make this Mass increase the congregation's faith in the power accruing to it here and now from the resurrection of Christ.

CHAPTER 33

Twelfth Sunday after Pentecost

Today's Mass is introduced with the invocation that we pray at the beginning of each of the hours of the Breviary. It is noteworthy that we repeat the same prayer, at least in substance, in the Collect, with special reference to the Mass about to be celebrated: "it is through your grace that the faithful are able to serve you fittingly and laudably." We should tell our congregations with all possible emphasis that they must indeed pray about this. For many are no longer vitally aware of the fact that the Mass is a *service* before and for God and that this service levies certain definite demands upon the mental and physical posture of the individual, for such a public business as the liturgy is shown by its own etymology to have been thought to be, cannot in any sense be the private affair of the individual. All of us reject with indignant disdain the old tenet: "Religion is a private matter." We rightly contend that it is entirely false. But how many have no scruples about treating the Mass in practice as their own private business, demanding that their private rubrics be respected and registering indignation or at least annoyance when admonished that they must accomodate thoughts, words and posture to the service about to be discharged in God's presence by his people as they celebrate the Mass they have been commissioned to solemnize. (The same holds analogously for the celebrant.)

What Paul says about the significance and glory of this service in the epistle is quite in the spirit of Introit and Collect.

He does indeed speak in the first instance of his own special apostolic service and ministry, but his words apply also to the ministry of the community. Of the ministerial office of the apostle and of the ministry of the community it must be said that we are not sufficient of ourselves to cope with it but "our sufficiency is from God. He also it is who has made us fit ministers of the new covenant," that is, no longer ministers of the dead letter that kills but rather ministers of the living and life-giving Spirit. Paul contrasts with the ministry of the Old Testament based upon the letter of the law the glory of the New Testament ministry in the apostolic office of preaching and liturgizing. Upon the tables brought down by Moses from the mountain of God was engraved the law which Paul says was "the ministration of death" and "the ministration that condemned" because as law it could not effect salvation. And yet, even in this ministration, which despite all its transitoriness was after all an encounter with God, the glory of God shone in transient transfiguration upon the face of Moses so that the Israelites dared not approach him until he had veiled his countenance.

How much more then must the "ministration that justifies" abound in glory! This applies to the liturgy of this congregation of ours, this Christian community, a liturgy in which Christ himself remits sins ("unto the forgiveness of sins" are the express words in the consecration of the chalice) in the rendering present of his salvific work and imparts grace, that is glory. How could we possibly frame such a ministry of our own power, did not God truly sustain us and render us capable of such exalted operation?

This is the place, therefore, to speak of the glory and magnificence of the liturgical ministry of the congregation; for it must be repeated that many churchgoers simply have no conception of this liturgical ministry of the laity; and whenever something is said to them about it, the response one always hears is: Why have we not been told this before? Why is this not preached about? On this Sunday we could make very weighty but also very inspiring remarks about the collaboration of the congregation in the liturgy; and we could appeal to St. Paul for confirmation of every word we would say. The Gradual also shows us with what joy we proclaim the praise of God in the liturgy when once we know what is really here involved.

The gospel provides us with a remarkable insight into these trains of thought so spontaneously suggested in ordered sequence by the texts of today's Mass. We call it the gospel of the good Samaritan and in so doing totally overlook the introductory passage, "Blessed are the eyes that see what you see! For I say to you, many prophets and kings" as representatives of the Old Covenant "have desired to see what you see, and they have not seen it." Christ is telling those around him that they are seeing and hearing things much more wonderful than those experienced by any of the great men of old and that therefore these contemporaries of Christ are to be called blessed. Are not these words the direct continuation of the epistle? The Old Testament pales altogether before the reality of the New. And what is this reality? Christ and the dawning of the new kingdom of God!

We should ask ourselves how we see this beatitude pronounced by Jesus and applicable to ourselves as well. What do our eyes see and our ears hear? From the human and earthly point of view, simply what each succeeding generation of mankind has experienced, if anything still more cruelty and grievous calamities. Is this beatitude pronounced by Christ going to get through to us in the liturgy: that is the crucial question of this Sunday's Mass. We must learn to realize our own blessedness as Church of Jesus Christ.

And these thoughts usher in still another noteworthy insight relative to the gospel. The fathers saw in the good Samaritan the Son of God who descended from the throne of the heavenly Father and became a stranger (Samaritan) among men as he ministered healing to mankind which had fallen among thieves. This divine Samaritan brings mankind to the inn of his Church and leaves the two coins of baptism and the Eucharist to nourish mankind until he returns. This is the patristic interpretation elaborated in the homily we read today in the Breviary, although the portion containing the interpretation is subsequent to the excerpts included in the Breviary. Such an interpretation of the parable of the good Samaritan brings it entirely into alignment with the revelations of the other texts of today's Mass. The ministry of the priest and the levite do not effect any salvation, which comes only with and from Christ who comes from above. He is the true Samaritan, whose constant assistance the Christian people continually experiences and will experience until his second coming; and this assistance is afforded in no negligible degree in the liturgy in which the Samaritan is truly our "neighbor" as nowhere else, for no one is so close to us as our head in heaven whose members we are.

Liturgical sacrifice is also mentioned in Offertory and Communion verse; the expressions are taken from the Old Testament but they clearly mediate the conviction that the culmination of all sacrifice lies in that sacrifice which we have here solemnized, from which issues our strength and our joy. The wine and oil here mentioned (in the Communion verse) echo the parable of the Lord.

Would that all who participate in the eucharistic rite this Sunday might fully grasp the blessedness that this rite mediates to them!

CHAPTER 34

Thirteenth Sunday after Pentecost

Even a cursory inspection of the texts of this Mass will show that they continue the main theme of last Sunday's Mass, using it as a point of departure for new insights and new precepts. It would be a good thing, perhaps at the very outset of the sermon, to recall briefly the theme of last Sunday's Mass, in order to make clear immediately the nexus between these two Sundays.

The contrast between the Old Covenant and the New again emerges clearly in the epistle. The law cannot bring salvation; salvation can be procured only through the one offspring of Abraham, through Christ to whom the promise has been made. There is no need to engage in any detailed treatment of the reasons adduced by St. Paul for the insufficiency and nullity of the Old Testament law; it suffices simply to stress the superiority of the New Testament dispensation. The people of the New Covenant then rightly utter the plea of the Introit, repeated word for word in the Gradual: "Advert to your covenant, O Lord!" It is fitting that the New Testament people of God pray him thus to look upon them and remember his covenant with them, for this new people of God are constantly and habitually dependent on the continually renewed influx of grace; for "the Scripture shut up all things under sin, that by the faith of Jesus Christ the promise might be given to those who believe." Redemption and salvation are not the fruit of boasting about personal achievements, not even of the punctilious fulfillment of the prescriptions of the law; they come from faith in Jesus Christ, from the faith of Jesus Christ, *ex fide Jesu Christi.*

What was theoretically proven in the epistle is portrayed as a concrete event in the gospel. Nine of the ten cured lepers fulfill their duty punctiliously; only one pierces through the shell of the law to the salvific kernel who is Christ himself, falls down before him and gives glory to God. And for this reason he is the only one to obtain not only the cure of his leprosy but salvation as well, because he believed. So likewise do all of our works remain unprofitable unless they are done in the faith which makes Christ ours and us his. The danger of spiritual bureaucracy is by no means surmounted among the heirs of the New Covenant; the fact that the only one to be mentioned in today's gospel as having surmounted it was a Samaritan, a foreigner, may well serve as a warning for the people of the New Testament.

This gospel is not concerned with the gratitude which politeness demands be shown in social life. The crucial point is the realization of where the true hope of health and salvation is to be found, whether in the scrupulous fulfillment of the letter of the law, or in the personal union of the Healer and Saviour. The danger of a false neo-Platonic objective idealism is clearly evident in the fact that many Christians are today outwardly living a scrupulously Christian life, endeavoring at every opportunity to promote the "cause of Christ" and of the Church, but betray, upon closer inspection, a total ignorance of the personal value of Christ and the Church, an ignorance virtually precluding any genuine personal relation to Christ or the Church. This problem points up the precariousness of the Christian existence of every one of us in this world. Again and again we are posed the task of piercing through all impersonal forms and formulations to the genuinely personal encounter with the one Christ, in which encounter alone our salvation is to be found. This applies to all the canonical and moral-theological dispositions of the Church; it applies also to liturgy. Never are we bound by an impersonal disposition; it is always rather by the personal operation of the Lord in the dispositions of his Church.

This encounter with Christ is the object of the petitions in Introit and Alleluia verse; but this encounter will be granted us only if these petitions are really the expression of our personal devotion. Nor should our sacrificial devotion be a mere impersonal ceremonial; it too must spring from real personal trust in the Lord. Even as we lay our gifts upon his altar, so do we place our destiny in his hands (Offertory). Only then do we come to know in faith how he answers our devotion with the bread from heaven "all savory and sweet to taste" (Communion). The sweetness of this bread, which we receive for other reasons than mere sense of duty or fidelity to the law, becomes for us a sign of all the other salvific ordinances and dispositions of God. We must learn to love them in order for them to lead us to the promises spoken of in the Collect and the epistle.

CHAPTER 35

Fourteenth Sunday after Pentecost

The motif proper to this Sunday's Mass is the contrast between the kingdom of God and the world. The aim of the Mass is to lead and guide the congregation, through participation in the solemnization of the work of Christ, the reception of his word and his sacrament, to an unequivocal choice of the kingdom of God in preference to the world. This kingdom of God is brought from the very outset before the eyes of the worshiping congregation as a goal of ardent desire. The entire Psalm 83 from which the Introit verses are taken expresses the longing of an exile for the sanctuary of home: "Better ... one day in your courts than a thousand elsewhere. ... How lovely is your dwelling place, O Lord of hosts." And this longing must be aroused in the Christian congregation of the twentieth century. The holy place, the temple, is the image of the coming glory of God; this is true not only of the Old Testament Temple but also of the New Testament place of worship. In this house of God stands "the anointed," the chosen people of God, upon whom gaze down the gracious and benevolent eyes of their divine Protector. This dwelling-place (*tabernaculum*) of God cannot yet be the abiding habitation of the people of God, for that people is still in the world, in a far country, in an alien land. (It should be noted that the original Latin *alienus*, from *alius*, had no pejorative sense; its semantic evolution is especially poignant for the theologico-psychological point here being made, for in fact any "land" or state or even legitimate concern which is not God is or should be, by that very fact, at best less attractive, at worst downright inimical.)

This tension between the call to domicile in the house of God and the dislodgment into the alien world with its threats and demands is clearly presented to the congregation in both Scripture readings in the words of divine revelation. The antitheses are Spirit and flesh (epistle), God and mammon (gospel). It would be an error to equate the Pauline contrast between Spirit and flesh with the contrast between spirit and matter in the sense of soul and body. Paul lists among the "works of the flesh" not only the excesses of sensuality originating from the bodily appetites but anger, enmity, and envy as well, which latter three have their seat in man's mental and spiritual life; conversely, Paul considers (bodily) continence and chastity as fruit of the Spirit.

It should be noted, incidentally, that Paul speaks of the "works" of the flesh but of the "fruit" of the Spirit. The grammatical number in each case is a pregnant indication respectively of the centrifugal turbulence to which the man living according to the flesh is exposed and into which he falls; and of the integral wholeness to which the Spirit leads him.

By the flesh Paul means the merely natural man as he came into existence on this earth "... from human stock ... from the will of the flesh ... from the will of man" (Jn 1, 13) and by his very entry into the world came under the power of sin. But this drive of the flesh challenges even him who is "born by spiritual birth ... a thing of spirit" (Jn 3, 6), although such an attack is unwarranted, since such a man is no longer a debtor to the flesh (cf. epistle, eighth Sunday after Pentecost). Should such a man yield to the flesh, then he forfeits the kingdom of God. If, however, he follows the Spirit, then he is no longer "under the Law," that is, he is no longer living under the law as an alien power, rather in the union he has with the Spirit, the very breath of the divine life, he is aware of his true freedom, even when, like "they who belong to Christ" he is crucifying his "flesh with its passions and desires."

An expansive paraphrase of St. Paul's expressions should thus be used, just as on the eighth Sunday after Pentecost, to bring the congregation to the realization that all its members have been elevated body and soul into the divine Spirit, so that they are now in that state of adoption in which they can cry, "Abba, Father" making them heirs of God and joint heirs with Christ.

This is all admittedly difficult to grasp. But this difficulty does not justify us in simply refraining from proclaiming any of it. On the contrary, precisely because it is difficult, we must be that much the more at pains to make this spiritual reality our own vital possession and to witness to it so fervently as to make the congregation—and ourselves—ever more aware of what it means to be a Christian. Only then will we acquire the capacity and the desire (Offertory) to live and act as Christians. It is no mere accident or coincidence that this is precisely the task that has been posed for us in every single epistle since the sixth Sunday after Pentecost.

The tension between Spirit and flesh comes out in the gospel in the contrast between God and mammon. The root meaning of mammon is those possessions which form the basis for a life of security but from the viewpoint of eternity prove a fraud since only God can give us security of tenure in the kingdom of God! Every man is somehow subject to one master; but if faced with two masters, he cannot but prefer (love) one and ignore and downgrade (hate) the other. Jesus invites the congregation to inspect the credentials of the two masters capable of deciding their fate. The impotence of mammon, the uselessness of worldly security, is proven in striking images: no amount of human industry or effort can extend the human body or the human life beyond its appointed span. Birds (spoken of also in vv. 4 f. of the same Psalm 83 from which the Introit is taken; they nest in the belfry and on the roof of the church!) and flowers direct the congregation to "the Father" as the *Abba Father* motif is suggested afresh.

Indeed this is the point at which we can most graphically signify when the invocation of the Father is genuine and when it is not. It is genuine when this appeal expresses a vital interior trust, a serene confidence without reserve or diminution. For the Father is a father in the fullest sense only if he knows and satisfies the real needs of his children. As long as we trust him only with reservations or imperfectly in this matter, we are not saying in the Spirit of true sonship that "Father" that we utter with our lips. This Spirit has not been granted to the pagans and so they do not know the Father and have naturally stumbled into the thankless service of the mammon of the world. Just as the pagans (the "gentiles" in the gospel) belong to mammon, so do the "sons" belong to the kingdom of God. This is their proper domain and must therefore be their prime concern.

This discourse of our Lord can show us the difference between serving the world and belonging to the kingdom of God, between doing the works of the flesh and showing forth (precisely to that same world) the fruit of the Spirit, a noble life in the sonship of God.

To this the Offertory summons us: we are to taste and see how good the Lord is and how safe we are in his keeping. In this disposition we then proceed to offer ourselves in the presentation of our gifts. And this is truly to seek the kingdom of God, here and now, before all other things.

CHAPTER 36

Fifteenth Sunday after Pentecost

The opposition between Spirit and flesh is once again presented to the worshiping congregation in today's Mass text. Note well the steadfast continuity. Some of the expressions are the same as those used last Sunday (cf. the epistle), while others differ in wording but convey the same meaning. Thus in the Secret, we have the contrast between the sacrament of the Lord and the attacks of the devil; in the Postcommunion, between the "working of this heavenly gift" and "our own inclinations." But the new emphasis in this Mass has been clearly set by the Collect, in which the congregation confesses that it, the Church, is dependent upon the abiding mercy of God in order to remain pure and inviolable, and prays therefore for the continual gift of divine guidance.

It would be useful to compile the statements made by the *ecclesia orans*, the praying Church, about herself; it would provide a substantial elaboration of the picture and therefore of the understanding of the Church over that presented by the *ecclesia docens*, the teaching Church. When the Church is speaking to men with divine commission and authority, the misunderstanding can occasionally arise that the Church is possessed of an autonomous warranty in matters involving God and man. The prayer of the praying Church in this Mass presents a different picture: the Church, as she appears in the individual parishes and in their sum total, knows her own weakness and insecurity, as long as she has only herself to depend on; only through the abiding

mercy and the gracious guidance of her Lord does she preserve
her purity and endure in safety.

The epistle shows how right and needful is such prayer and
petition: for the opposition between Spirit and flesh holds not
only for the generic sphere of humanity but even in the company
of the faithful itself. In the Church herself, the "vain ambitions"
more proper to the world outside may be indulged; within the
Church can arise mutual provocation and mutual ill-will, envy and
jealousy. All of these are "works of the flesh" even in the Church,
the community of God, formed and built in the Spirit. And such
jealousies, ill-will and mutual provocation may arise not only between individuals but also in the relations between ecclesiastical
institutions, church groups, ecclesiastical offices. The history of the
Church provides ample evidence of each of these works of the
flesh. Who would dare to maintain that there is not and cannot
be any of this nowadays? The Pauline admonition and warning is
trenchant and unmistakable: Make no mistake about it; you cannot cheat God. And the meaning is surely this: do not misuse or
scorn the Spirit, do not attempt to manage without that Spirit,
like the deluded one who "thinks himself to be something, whereas
he is nothing," for this is self-deception and, worse still, an effort
to cheat God by slighting his Spirit and still aiming at holiness!

And so it may also be the case in the congregation, in the
parish, in the Church, that some "sow in the flesh" and "reap
corruption." The very grave question must therefore be asked as
to how matters stand with this "sowing in the flesh," not among
pagans who do not know God but right inside the Church herself.
Have there been periods when the Church sowed in the flesh? Are
there furrows for such "sowing in the flesh" in the internal and
external affiliations and alliances of the Christian congregations?
In menacing situations it can of course be productive of very unpleasant consequences for a congregation of Christians to refrain
from sowing in the flesh and instead trust in the Spirit. But only in
the Spirit is eternal life to be harvested, even in periods of chaotic
confusion and disparagement of the spiritual as unworldly and

unrealistic, unprogressive and unmodern, and the like. The point is quite simply that the real strength and support of the Christian community and congregation come not from the flesh but rather from the unity of individuals in the Spirit, whose fruit as described in this epistle is distinguished by mildness, modesty, selflessness and love.

The verses of the Gradual and Alleluia, usually to be considered as the reaction of the congregation to the hearing of the word of God, show us what the congregation has absorbed from that word of God as read today: It is good to praise God in a hymn that proclaims his mercy and his faithfulness; God alone is the supreme Lord and King over all the earth. In a lenten ferial Mass can be found the words of the prophet Jeremias, which might be termed the other side of the same coin: "Cursed shall he be ... that puts his trust in man, and will have flesh and blood to aid him (Jer 17, 5). Such a contraposition will serve to bring out the full gravity of these verses and of the epistle itself.

The gospel can be readily fitted into these trains of thought, especially when it is borne in mind that the central character in the miracle at Naim is actually the mother of the deceased young man. The fathers have therefore seen in this mother who "was a widow," alone and forsaken in the world, the Church whom Christ meets to restore to her her dead children. The sons that have sown in the flesh and reaped death arise to new life when Christ visits his people. And so the content of this event in Naim is the destiny of the Church, our own destiny. The Church waits today also for the Lord to visit his people; and visit them he does, collectively and individually, in this most solemn mystic rite.

And so it is of quite immediate significance that the congregation, revivified by the word of God just proclaimed to the whole community of worshipers, confidently takes up in the Offertory the "new song," that God has put into their mouth, and sings a hymn of their God. Even as they sing, the worshipers are well aware of their constant battle with temptation in this world and of the insufficiency of all earthly ambition and desire. But they receive "the bread" of which the Lord says it is "my Flesh for the life of the world" (Communion). And even here his word holds true: "only the Spirit gives life; the flesh is of no avail" (Jn 6, 64). And so the opposition between Spirit and flesh can penetrate even to the innermost mystery of the Church. How important it is for the Church to reckon with this possibility and how necessary for her to recognize and expose the contention of the flesh against the Spirit.

CHAPTER 37

Sixteenth Sunday after Pentecost

The epistle is without any doubt the most sharply and clearly defined portion of today's Mass text, both in form and in content. In comparison with it, the other texts display a certain generality of tone which must be concretized from the standpoint of the epistle.

The chief content of the epistle is a prayer of the great St. Paul for his congregation, of the apostle to the gentiles for the Church. This gives the epistle in today's Mass a special significance for the pastor. Paul speaks in most solemn tones, as it were before his congregation to "the Father . . . from whom all fatherhood in heaven and on earth receives its name" or, in simpler terms, to the Father of all angels and men. In this solemn discourse—a true *oratio*—he tells the Father whither he would like to guide his congregation, his community of Christians, what is the essential aim of his pastoral activity.

In this context there arise several questions of importance for pastoral and parochial work today. The questions grow out of the observation of pastoral action in our time which seems to me to suffer very often from a certain aimlessness and lack of spiritual purposefulness. How many parish priests today have a clear picture of what they want to make out of their congregation, out of the community of Christians entrusted to their care? Is the aim really still a genuine interior "molding" of the community of worshipers? Or does actual parish work today not rather consist in many cases of a more or less casual and disconnected series of "devotional exercises"? Does the motley series of holy hours, May devotions, lenten and advent services really aim at genuine religious "education," at the molding of an integral attitude of piety, of a relationship to God in Christ? Or does all of this amount to nothing more than an occasional religious exercise for the Christian community?

What are Paul's petitions for his congregation? I would assume that he makes the same petitions today for the entire Church, even if such petitions strike us nowadays as strange in the midst of the giddiness of this age of ours. The individual petitions of this great prayer deserve careful meditation:

1. "... to be strengthened with power," yes, and for what reason? "... unto the progress of the inner man." And how? "through his [God's] Spirit"! What is the application of this to pastoral activity, the celebration of the Eucharist, the administration of the sacraments, the proclamation of the word? How should we here construct our examination of conscience? Well, it would be good to ask ourselves at the conclusion of a Mass if that Mass was so celebrated in general and in every particular as to enable the entire congregation to absorb, if they were receptive, some of that power for the inner man that comes from the Spirit of God. It would be good if we put ourselves the question: are we motivated, even in the slightest degree, in the celebration of the Mass, by the desire to mediate a spiritual molding and formation of the faithful, a training that is expressed even in externals (dignity, a measured pace, avoidance of all bustle, a perfect harmony of word and action on the part of the celebrant and between celebrant and congregation)?

2. "... to have Christ dwelling through faith in your hearts." Here we must put to ourselves the same questions as above, but primarily this question: Are we still aware, in our pastoral activity, of the difference between simply "believing in Jesus Christ" and what Paul has here in mind, namely that keen awareness of Christ's presence within us, in the true act of faith and, above all, in the attitude, posture and habit of faith?

3. Points 1 and 2 above should, according to Paul, lead the Christian community to be rooted and grounded with their whole being in love; and this ontological rooting and grounding should in turn further lead the community to gain "gnosis," supernaturally mediated comprehension for Christ's naturally unfathomable love for us. So the course is set: from power to faith through which Christ becomes present to us in the fullness of his personality, and then to the gnosis of love, in which is consummated the final perfection of the Christian community: "filled unto all the fullness of God." This is the picture of a true Christian community, of a genuine congregation and company of the *faithful*; this is the goal the apostle sets himself with the help of grace. How does our own "practical" pastoral activity check out against this model?

If today, on this Sunday, a pastor would discuss all this before his congregation and would say quite simply, without purple prose or highflown phrases: this is the way St. Paul pictures his congregation, this is the way he pictures the Church; this is what I, too, would like you to become; so I will pray for you even as Paul for his congregation; and it is my desire to bring Christ close to you in such a way, to help you in such a way that his power, his love will become your interior possession, so that you may attain to that marvelous state described by Paul at the end of his prayer, "filled unto all the fullness of God"—if a pastor would speak in this vein, could not such a sermon represent a genuine inception of communal training and of forming the *congregation* (*grex*: "flock") into a true *community* (*communitas*: "fellowship")? And would not this process lead to a more meaningful commerce between pastor and congregation as well? Should we not risk it, precisely in this Sunday's Mass? Our reward would be the genesis of communities of worshipers to whom is truly applicable the last great phrase of Paul's prayer: "to him be glory *in the Church* and *in Christ Jesus* down through all the ages of time without end." It seems to me both genuinely useful and mandatory that we check out our entire pastoral work against this model and order it anew.

The last sentence of the epistle "to him be glory in the Church and in Christ Jesus" is taken up in the Gradual by a congregation fully aware of its meaning: All the kings of the earth stand reverently before the glory of God, who has built up Sion, his Church, in order to manifest in her his glory—exactly the substance of Paul's prayer. And in this spirit the community of worshipers intones the "new canticle" celebrating the wondrous works of God. Today the congregation should intone that song in a special access of fervor, since it has learned of God's splendid designs for his flock, for *this* community, *this* congregation. The worshipers experience personally how "gentle and lenient" is the God whose mercy and compassion they have invoked upon themselves (Introit). They see his compassion anew in the gospel where the Lord, in fulfillment of the true spirit of the Sabbath (cf. Mt 12, 12 and Lk 13, 16), imparts healing to the man with dropsy, a type of the human being bloated with pride, and then warns that grace and glory can be won only in humility. The splendid destiny portrayed in the epistle is the sure reward only of the man "who humbles himself"; such a man, and *only* such a man, does God exalt to the heights which Paul prays that his congregation may achieve.

Molded in this humility, in no small measure also by the endurance of hostile machinations but always in the expectation of the help of our Lord, the worshipers enter into his sacrifice (Offertory) and learn how he alone with his "matchless justice" provides a solid bulwark for the whole of our lives (Communion): a bulwark in the power and love and fullness of the spirit of Christ, even as Paul has petitioned for the Church and as we are resolved to pray on this present Sunday and hereafter as well in those same words of St. Paul.

CHAPTER 38

Seventeenth Sunday after Pentecost

The Introit of today's Mass provides an excellent nexus with last Sunday's, in which the congregation professed God so unreservedly to be the very foundation of their being (Communion verse). Today the worshipers begin with the same solemn profession: "You are just, O Lord, and your judgment is right. Deal with your servant according to your compassion" (Introit). The epistle crystallizes one such judgment of the Lord: he has "called" the congregation of the faithful, *this* congregation. This truth must be presented very graphically today to the congregation: they have a calling. Last Sunday's epistle could be used in order to briefly portray this calling in detail once again. In any case, it must be explained quite clearly to every congregation just what it means to be "called," not just at the end of their lives but right this minute, in this very Mass, this very act of worship. The more exalted the vocation we have received from God, the humbler, the more forbearing we ought to be, the more "careful to preserve the unity of the Spirit in the bond of peace." This is of great importance for the Christian calling, for this calling is no mere isolated affair of the individual; the individual is rather called as a member of the community which the Spirit has been sustaining since Pentecost. To be in communion with the apostles, with the Church, means to be in communion with the Father and his Son, Jesus Christ (cf. 1 Jn 1, 3).

In this community are hidden the standards to which we are

called, not only as "one spirit" but also as one body, as a visible community. Hence there must be visible community in prayer and worship as well. The spirit determines the physical posture and stance of the congregation, their audible words and their song. How manifold is the foundation of the unity of this *community* of worshipers: "one hope ... one Lord, one faith, one baptism, one God and Father of all." So numerous, so powerful and so closely knit are the factors producing this unity and so stunning is the sight of this unity that the enumeration finally merges, as last Sunday's did, into a song of praise to the one "Father of all."

The worshiping community of Christians thereupon recognizes itself, full of exultation, in this exuberance and splendor: "Blessed the nation whose God is the Lord, the people he has chosen for his inheritance." But the worshipers also confess humbly that they owe everything solely to the power and compassion of this Lord of theirs, to whom ascends their earnest supplication (Gradual and Alleluia verse). Do our congregations today still retain any sense of being, even as they stand there at Mass in their several churches, this *beata gens*, this "people chosen for God's inheritance?" Is it not a crying shame if this fact remains hidden from them because we have not proclaimed it, have not proclaimed it this very day, this very Sunday?

What indeed does it mean to be a "Christian people"? Is it a group like the pharisees who ask after the law and put very searching questions concerning the status and hierarchy of the commandments? Certainly such a question is an important one. And Jesus answers it. But he then puts a quite different question himself, a question that goes far beyond the law as such: "What do you think of the Christ?" What and who is he? The Christ who brings salvation, who as David's Lord founds that kingdom of which David's was but an obscure foreshadowing? This Christ, his masterpiece, his very kingdom, is the community of worshipers he has called and given his own name. The Christ-question is the primordial and the crucial one; only in the wake of a proper answer to that question can the right answer be given to all other questions of religion and morality. Do our congregations these days still realize this fact that they must always first put the question as to Christ, his meaning, his power and his kingdom? Blessed the people whom this Christ brings to the Father as his chosen inheritance!

In the eucharistic sacrifice we testify to our sentiments, as a Christian community, concerning Christ. Daniel's prayer (Offertory) is presently fulfilled upon this worshiping congregation of Christians: God's countenance shines in splendor over this sanctuary, over this people, this congregation, in which the Lord is rendered present because his name "is invoked upon this people." In the eucharistic sacrifice the congregation of worshipers comes to know the sovereign power of this Christ whom David calls his Lord; and in the Communion verse this community of Christians proclaims that power after receiving his body. To him who is above every king upon earth belongs every congregation of the faithful, for he has called them by his sovereign word. And so every congregation of Christian worshipers, even the one that celebrates its Eucharist in the remotest little village of some mission territory, is truly a *beata gens* if only that congregation answers aright, in heart and soul, the question: "What do you think of the Christ?"

CHAPTER 39

The Eschatological Sundays

Every Mass is fundamentally eschatologically oriented, inasmuch as it points by its very nature to that definitive and indefectible state of salvation which in the interim can only be represented in ephemeral signs and tokens. Especially in the Postcommunions, the worshiping congregation of the faithful is repeatedly oriented to the eschatological consummation of their state and status. But in the long line of Sundays after Pentecost the last ones, beginning with the eighteenth, can readily be shown to have specially pronounced eschatological features.

CHAPTER 40

Eighteenth Sunday after Pentecost

The Introit begins with the prayer: "Grant peace, O Lord, to those who wait for you, that your prophets may be found faithful." This might be considered at first glance to be simply a general pious petition. But the peace for which the Church is praying is never simply a civic concern any more than it is simply a matter of the individual having a good and quiet conscience. Peace in the sense of the Church's petition is rather that peace "which the world cannot give"; it is that state and condition, in which every one and everything in the entire world, in the whole created universe, has reached such a final fulfillment and consummation that every existent being is so fully satisfied and secure as to be impervious to the very thought of self-enrichment by means of injury or vexation to another. In this sense, Christian peace is synonymous with the full revelation of the Kingdom of God. This interpretation of the Introit petition emerges from the epistle, in which the unmistakable theme is the enrichment and fulfillment of the company of the faithful enabling them to await the appearance of their Lord Jesus Christ who keeps them secure in this expectation against the great day of his coming.

It is precisely the proper appreciation in faith of the riches and blessedness procured by Christ's redemptive work for the company of the faithful in his Church which will incline the congregation to long for that state that guarantees it the manifestation of those riches and their definitive inviolability. Hence, too, the eschatological orientation of the words of the Gradual: "I rejoiced at the tidings which were told me, 'We shall go into the house of the Lord.' " The house of the Lord is for the congregation at this Sunday's Mass no longer the temple in Jerusalem nor even the Christian house of worship but rather the eschatological manifestation of that house of the Lord in the New Jerusalem. The congregation today is expressly set on its way thither by the succeeding Gradual verse that speaks of the peace and plenteousness of the Holy City, where the company of the faithful, including *this* congregation, will be able to participate in the ineffable triumph of him whose glory they share in receiving his body and whom all the kings of the earth will on that great day praise and serve in reverent awe.

The gospel of the paralytic and his miraculous cure seems at first glance not to fit into this patently eschatological context. But it must be remembered that every one of Christ's miracles of healing is of its very nature a foreshadowing of the eschatological restoration in glory of the human body. The Lord does not work his miracles as a mere medicine man but rather as the one who wills to reveal in his glory the new man, the new heavens and the new earth. This salvific will of Jesus is attested by every miracle of healing. But the miracle related in today's gospel points up especially the intimate nexus between forgiveness of sins and bodily healing and thereby renders present precisely in the healed paralytic that eschatological perfection of man in which the worshiping community is here participating already in this mystic rite.

The congregation so participating in these holy mysteries thus sees itself on the one hand as filled with the life of God and therefore consummated, and on the other hand as still shackled in a kind of transitoriness from which the worshipers beg with special fervor to be delivered precisely because of the glorious vision they have of the splendor of their final state. Thus do they offer like Moses an "evening sacrifice" (Offertory), because for them the evening of the world has come. A splendid and striking phrase of the Secret pinpoints the significance of this sacrifice: "O

God, who by the august exchange (*veneranda commercia*) of this sacrifice dost make us partakers of the one supreme Godhead ..." From this realization stems the joyous self-exhortation of the Communion verse to surrender to the Lord as a sacrifice and so to enter into the glory of his everlasting courts.

The spiritual benefit of this sacrificial rite ought therefore to issue into a firm will to attain to this consummation and a longing expectation of the great day of Christ's return; for that day will truly bring with it the fullness of salvation for the Christian community and for the whole world.

CHAPTER 41

Nineteenth Sunday after Pentecost

In this Sunday's Mass, the tragic course of the marriage feast, as portrayed in the gospel, should rivet our attention. What confusion do we find in this parable of Our Lord! We are told of a splendid royal marriage feast, a great event to which one would think anybody would be proud and delighted to be invited—but the invited guests balk at coming. The invitation to the wedding elicits the bewildering response of murder, punished in turn by the extermination of an entire city. But the wedding feast must go on notwithstanding; messengers are dispatched anew with invitations, more insistent this time; the banquet hall is full of guests and the expectation is that the story will at last have a happy festive ending. But no! The brilliance of the marriage feast pales entirely before the fate of the one man who has no wedding garment and is cast forth into the darkness outside where there is weeping and gnashing of teeth. Such is the sad outcome of the invitation to the royal marriage feast.

Could any marriage feast have such appalling attendant circumstances? Yes, the marriage of the Son of God with the race of man he came to redeem! This marriage feast, this partnership of love, was announced by the prophets; it began with the incarnation in the womb of the Virgin, proceeded historically through the death on Calvary and the resurrection, and will be consummated by the return of the divine partner at the end of time. But we know that this marriage feast has become a stumbling block and pitfall for so many, the occasion of eternal perdition for the hosts of those who, distracted by the joys and sorrows of this world, have been unwilling to participate in the banquet or have tried to crash it without even donning that wedding garment which is the complimentary gift of their host.

Faced so clearly with the solemn and awful warning of that last great day when the thoughts of many hearts shall be revealed, we could only despair did we not hear in the Introit the Lord's own assurance: "I am the salvation of the people . . . in whatever distress they shall cry to me, I will hear them; and I will be their Lord forever." This comforting assurance encourages us to accept undaunted the admonition of the epistle to "put on the new man, which has been created according to God in justice and holiness of truth." And so we send up our prayer anew to God in the Gradual and prepare ourselves afresh for the "evening" sacrifice.

In the power of this sacrifice we know that, though we walk in the midst of tribulations, God will give us life and will save us despite all the assaults of the enemy (Offertory).

Again made partakers of the marriage feast through the reception of the body of Christ, we pray the more insistently (Communion verse) that we may preserve our God-given justification, the wedding garment, on all the winding roads of this life until the last great call comes to us and we are summoned to be partakers of the royal wedding feast made manifest.

This Sunday's Mass is therefore an important and valuable supplementation of the understanding of the eschatological situation mediated to us by last Sunday's texts.

CHAPTER 42

Twentieth Sunday after Pentecost

Today the congregation assembled for Mass must surely be quite surprised to hear itself saying that it is sitting by the rivers of Babylon and weeping at the memory of the city of Sion (Offertory). What have our present-day congregations to do with the grieving Jews in Babylon? But a little reflection on the two preceding Sundays' Masses shows us that these words are a most telling description of the situation of the Christian people. The Church is the chosen people of the New Covenant but she must continue to live in exile. She sits in this world and thinks of the glory promised her in the New Jerusalem to come. She experiences in this world all the hardships and vicissitudes of exile in her constant clashes and altercations with the children and the rulers of this world who are often far more powerful and worldly-wise than she. Even before hearing the Offertory, the congregation has expressed its own situation in the Introit in a way that is fully in accord with the sentiments of the Offertory: "All that you have done to us, O Lord, you have done in just judgment, because we have sinned against you and disobeyed your commandments." These words evaluate the crimes of the powers of this dispensation not from the standpoint of ecclesiastical politics but rather from the standpoint of *salvation history*. And so we must not apply these words to periods of salvation history which are already past. We are talking about our own situation and we must realize that these words refer to this situation of ours, otherwise the great texts of today's Mass will be rendered ineffective in advance. But we may take comfort, for the Lord will save us for the honor of his own name and will deal with us in accord with his "bounteous mercy" (Introit). Certainly "the days are evil"; but the power of the Spirit given to us enables us to triumph in spiritual joy over the wickedness of the times (epistle). This joy and exultation imparted to us with the spirit embolden us to raise our eyes to the Lord who will give us nourishment and help in due season (Gradual), if only our heart be ready in every possible situation to praise him in spiritual songs as our abiding glory.

And so we are like the royal official of whom the gospel speaks. For he too is traveling an anxious and troubled road, truly in the shadow of death. His hope is fixed solely upon the word that the Lord has spoken to him, "Thy son lives." In trusting confidence in this word of Christ does the nobleman depart. And we too, after we have received the body of our Lord, will have no other mainstay than the word with which the Lord has given us hope. This word will be our only consolation when this world humiliates us and our only support when this world weighs heavily upon us, so long as we sit by the rivers of Babylon and wait in expectant faith for the salvation of the New Jerusalem. Still another aspect of the eschatological posture and attitude of mind, which demands of us the wisdom of faith!

CHAPTER 43

Twenty-first Sunday after Pentecost

More somber still is the picture of the last days painted for us by the texts of this Sunday's Mass. Again we can use the Offertory as the point of departure for its interpretation, that Offertory in which the just sufferer Job in his utter ruin and extremity in the land of the heathen becomes the type of the worshiping Christian community. From this catastrophe of Job, stark tragedy from the human point of view, we gain a proper understanding of the gospel of the wicked servant. Our Lord's own summing up does indeed put the stress on the necessity of mutual forgiveness and forbearance. But within the framework of this Sunday's Mass as a whole, the stress lies more on the frightful perversity with which the wicked man can throttle and torment his fellow men. The wicked servant's conduct toward his fellow servant is truly monstrous and shocking.

That such things can happen is shown by the fate of Job. That they can happen to us and will indeed happen to us in the last days is revealed to us by the epistle. The Christian company of the faithful will have it harder in those last days than the throttled servant or Job, because that company of faithful has to fight not only "against flesh and blood ... but with malign influences in an order higher than ours" whose henchmen on earth the Apocalypse tells us will oppress and vanquish the saints upon earth (Ap 13, 7). And we shall not escape. The Lord has spoken of such tribulations too often and here, where the worshiping community is being deliberately prepared for the last days, the apostle speaks about them quite openly. But he also intimates to us that this struggle is not a hopeless one for us, if only we make proper use of our God-given armor: truth and justice, which are gifts of God; the power that streams from the gospel of peace; the shield of faith; and the weapons that lie ready at hand in the shape of our trust in his saving power and will and in the promises of God (epistle). Furthermore, the Lord is our king to whom we offer this Mass as homage; and he is the master of every situation, of ours as of Job's, as of that of the oppressed servant, as of that of the Jewish people in the days of Esther, whose words we appropriate in the Introit to profess our faith in the absolute sovereign majesty of God even in time of oppression. This same faith we profess in the Gradual as well, where we recall the power of God by which Israel was once delivered out of Egypt (Alleluia verse). And we, who are oppressed as was Israel, as was Job in the land of the heathen, as was the servant in the Gospel, find thereupon in Communion the salvation of our God and combine with this discovery in the Communion verse our earnest prayer that the evil days may be shortened.

CHAPTER 44

Twenty-second Sunday after Pentecost

Our Lord's answer in this Sunday's gospel to the challenge of a decision between emperor and God, between Caesar and Christ, has a deeper meaning than simply that of a political principle for the regulation of the relations of the chosen people of both Old and New Covenants to the secular authorities. The people of Christ is a free people, the freest in the whole world, because to this people has been given the freedom of the sons of God. And so this people is basically not dependent upon other powers nor yet substantially subject to them. The Jewish people held fast in theory to its freedom in God but in practice compromised again and again with the powers of this world. A witness to such compromise is the denarius coin the Pharisees take out of their money-bag. Against this background the words of Christ, "Render ... to Caesar the things that are Caesar's and to God the things that are God's," reveal a deeper sense that might be expressed like this: Leave to the lord of this world his booty and turn in glorious, sovereign single-mindedness to God, your undoubted liege lord whose people you are!

The Church of Christ will be faced in the last days by such exceedingly difficult decisions (difficult, that is, from the human point of view); the Apocalypse is most explicit and instructive on this point. The expectation of such distress and affliction would certainly drive Christians into a perfect panic of anxiety; did not Paul proclaim to them: "I am convinced that the Lord Jesus who has begun a good work in you will bring it to perfection until the day of Christ Jesus." But these same Christians, even though reassured, must realize how important it is for them, in preparation for such grim and evil days to grow more and more in love, "in knowledge and in all discernment." Then they will be able "to approve the better things," they will be "filled with the fruit of justice through Jesus Christ," and it will be granted to them at the end to celebrate his great day "to the glory and praise of God" (epistle). In the fraternal community of the chosen people, that is in the Church, they will know in their hearts, even in days of affliction and persecution the power of God, their "helper and protector" (Gradual). But all of this they can expect only from the compassionate and merciful God who does not "mark iniquities" nor remember the sins of his people (Introit).

In the mingled shock and consolation of such insights, the community of worshipers initiates the sacrificial rite this Sunday once again with the words of Esther, looking up to the Lord, who rules over all earthly powers and is able to put into the mouths of his faithful the right words in the presence of their enemies. This trust dominates the attitude of the congregation also in the Communion. And so the worshipers pray in conclusion in the Communion verse: "I cry to you, for you will answer me, O God ..."

CHAPTER 45

Twenty-third Sunday after Pentecost

Only a congregation whose eschatological attitude has been molded by the active participation in the Masses of the preceding Sundays will experience the great consolation proclaimed by the prophet in the Introit of the twenty-third Sunday after Pentecost. Speaking to his people in the name of God, Jeremias cries: "I think thoughts of peace and not of affliction ... I will bring you back from captivity from all places." And this is the abiding promise of God.

This promise graphically illumines the words of the epistle. The apostle contrasts the Christians with those whose God is their belly, who behave as enemies of the cross of Christ and whose end will therefore surely be ruin and eternal perdition. But of the Christian Paul says: "Our citizenship [not our "commerce"!] is in heaven, from which also we eagerly await a Saviour, our Lord Jesus Christ who will refashion the body of our lowliness, conforming it to the body of his glory by exerting the power by which he is able also to subject all things to himself." Such a hope and expectation, accepted on faith, enables the congregation to stand fast in the Lord, even amid the demonic tumults of the last days. What is true of the fellow-workers of the apostle is true also of all who in their place and in their tradition labor in the service of that same gospel: "Their names are in the book of life."

Such a message moves the congregation to look serenely beyond all affliction and tribulation and accept the consummated redemption as a present fact in the exultation of the Gradual: "You have freed us from those who afflict us, O Lord, and you have put to shame those who hate us. In God will we glory all the day and praise your name forever." The darkness of the present time does indeed descend again for a moment in the Alleluia verse: "Out of the depths I cry to you, O Lord . . ." These depths have been plumbed in the story of the sorely smitten Job, of Esther's oppressed people, of the mishandled and throttled servant, of the chosen people in the Babylonian captivity; these depths are our own depths, the depths into which the Church is plunged in this dispensation.

The promise of the epistle finds its confirmation in the miracles of the Lord reported in today's gospel; these miracles are wrought upon two women who are clearly types of the Church. The Lord's own people find salvation in the midst of the clamorous world, amid the noisy crowd, as they touch the hem of his garment in the sacramental tokens. And so this people of Christ will arise out of the depths (Offertory) and hear, as they receive the body of the Lord, the promise that their petition tendered in faith will be fulfilled (Communion verse), that great petition for imperishable glory.

CHAPTER 46

Sixth (Transferred) Sunday after Epiphany

In the cycle of most of the Church's years, the sixth Sunday after Epiphany, which was not celebrated during that season, has its prayers and readings inserted between the twenty-third Sunday after Pentecost and the last Sunday of the Church year, with the other Propers of the twenty-third Sunday after Pentecost retained. Thus the congregation persists, in the reading of these inserted texts, in the same eschatological frame of mind to which it has been molded by the recent Sundays, from the eighteenth on; and the readings and prayers taken over from the sixth Sunday after Epiphany impart new strength and firmness to this eschatological attitude. There is a very good reason for the adaptability of these texts to the end of the Church's year: the Epiphany season is entirely eschatologically oriented as is indeed the feast itself which has a more eschatological character than almost any other feast of the Church's year. These eschatological Sundays can indeed be said to press beyond the season of Advent to the Epiphany of the Lord, his visible coming; it is simply that this mighty event is being celebrated and experienced under varying aspects. The coming of Christ brings for the world and mankind precisely both final undreamed-of shocks and ultimate unhoped-for salvation. Christians must be prepared for both in the last days. But every

Christian community of worshipers on this Sunday in this Mass is a type of those Christians of the last days.

It is that company of the faithful who, like the community to which Paul addressed the epistle read this Sunday, looks back with a heart full of gratitude upon the power of that gift of faith which has been theirs and simultaneously reviews the tribulations suffered and survived in love and in the buoyant power of hope. The paradox of the Christian life is expressed by St. Paul in one of his customary compact formulas: "... receiving the word [of God] in great tribulation, with joy of the Holy Spirit." And this is truly the state of the congregation assisting at this Sunday's Mass. God's word, even when received in great tribulation, brings with it the joy of the new life in the Spirit.

This we should try to make clear to the congregation before us. This community of worshipers must learn from sermon and liturgical celebration what it means to receive the word of God, here and now, to receive and accept that word in a world of hate, cruelty, oppression and persecution; and the impact of these two realities ought in fact to produce for this congregation the "joy of the Holy Spirit."

That is the only infallible indication that the eschatological exercise of this Sunday has been meaningfully accomplished. Of assistance here is the apostle's closing admonition: "... to await from heaven Jesus, his [God's] son, whom he [the Father] raised from the dead, who has delivered us from the wrath to come," *does* deliver us in this mystic rite, in which he certifies us as "beloved and chosen of God."

How admirably the Gradual echoes this revelation of the mystery of the Christian community which confesses, in this text, its own mysterious destiny.

This mysterious destiny is confirmed by the gospel, as its final phrase clearly indicates. What has been "hidden since the foundation of the world," Christ has openly proclaimed: the victory of the little flock, that flock that seemed lost and forsaken, that flock which, like the tree that has grown from the tiny mustard seed shelters the birds of the air [all the peoples of the earth] in its branches, the flock which, like the leaven buried in the flour, leavens the whole lump [decides the fate of the world]. "Fear not, little flock, [although there is reason enough to fear!] for it is your father's good pleasure to give you the Kingdom" (Lk 12, 32). And the congregation will endorse this in the Communion verse, "Amen I say to you, all things whatsoever you ask for in prayer, believe that you shall receive, and it shall be done to you."

CHAPTER 47

Last Sunday after Pentecost

The opening adverb of the epistle might well serve as a motto for the overcoming of the eschatological tribulations: "unceasingly." It is perseverence which is required in order to endure the Gethsemanes and Armageddons of those days, which the Lord will permit to come upon his Church. In this perseverant expectation the community of Christians grows into the knowledge of the will of God, bears fruit in every good work and is completely strengthened through his glorious power unto perfect patience and long-suffering, can joyfully render thanks to God even in dark days for having "made us worthy to share the lot of the saints in light . . . transferred us into the kingdom of his beloved Son." All of this is confirmed anew in the words of the Lord in the gospel. He is speaking in the first instance of the immediately imminent destruction of Jerusalem; but his gaze travels beyond this event to the still greater and more oppressive burdens that will be the lot of his people in the last days, of which Jerusalem's doom was but a prelude. But even as he rescued his chosen ones from the collapse of Jerusalem, so will he also rescue his chosen ones in those last days and lead them into the new and eternal Jerusalem.

We have all had repeated occasion to observe to what a great extent the knowledge concerning the last days and their heavy responsibilities has been pushed into the background of the minds of Christians in our days. Yet we also know how necessary it is to think about these matters. These Sundays after Pentecost are

intended to make Christian worshipers capable of a proper eschatological attitude. And it should here be borne in mind that every
age in salvation history has in it elements of the last days; that
includes our own age. And so the practice of an eschatological
attitude is no mere theoretical exercise; it is rather an essential
and mandatory concern of integral Christian living.

CHAPTER 48

First Sunday of Advent

EYES UPON THE LORD OF GLORY

There is no sharp break between the series of eschatological Masses we have been celebrating since the eighteenth Sunday after Pentecost and the Advent season; rather there is continuity in form and content. The orientation is the same but the prospects become richer and more cheering.

The key eschatological event is the second coming of Christ. The primary effect of this second coming is the consummation of salvation, the secondary effect (not to be neglected however) is the last judgment. The texts of the eschatological Masses provide ample indication that they are intended to give the company of the faithful a clear picture of the final agony of the last days and practice in the eschatological attitude which will enable them to endure and survive the affliction and persecution certain to occur at that time. For whoever endures is victor once and for all over the frustrated attacker. Each and every Christian generation is summoned at the end of the Church's year to this "eschatological practice."

Advent is also a season of eschatological practice. We ought repeatedly to draw the attention of our congregations to the fact that "Advent" signifies not just any coming but, in a very special way, the coming of the Lord in glory. *Adventus* is the Latin term for the Greek *epiphaneia* which signifies the public appearance of the majesty of the Caesar or of God. And so the Church aims her Advent Masses at the same splendid proclamation of the second coming of Christ which terminated the series of the eschatological Sundays. The tradition followed in the account in St. Luke's gospel is not unaware of the terrors of the last days but these terrors are not so minutely portrayed as in St. Matthew's account, read on the last Sunday after Pentecost. And the more benign bias of the entire gospel of St. Luke introduces into the eschatological picture a new element which accordingly entirely dominates the Mass of this first Sunday of Advent: "But when these things begin to come to pass (namely the calamities preceding the appearance of the Son of man), look up and lift up your heads, because your redemption is at hand." The congregation echoes this sentiment with the *ad te levavi animam meam* of Introit and Offertory. But this *levavi animam meam* seems to me, despite the verbal similarity, to mean something different from the *levate capita vestra* of the gospel. The *levare animam meam* is not an expression of trusting confidence but rather an expression for the total self-surrender in the eucharistic sacrifice. In this sacrifice the gifts are "elevated" to God, for which action Martin Buber introduces in his translation the technical term *darhöhen* (literally, "to bring up" to God).[1] We have here then

---

[1] This Buber neologism has obviously been constructed on an analogy with the standard German verb "darbringen," which is "to offer," literally, "to bring *there*" (or, even better, *thither*). This verb expresses adequately the (exterior and interior) motion involved, but is too linear for Buber's purpose, not sufficiently evocative of the *upsurge*, of the vertical ascendant movement involved in the offering of the holy gifts. Therefore Buber compounds *darhöhen*, whose prefix *dar* retains the sense of movement lost in the prefix *er* of *erhöhen* ("exalt," the standard verb which he is replacing), while its stem *höhen* is clearly evocative of the upward movement, the *lifting up* of the gifts. The *dar* prefix indeed has overtones even richer and more evocative liturgically than those of mere movement, for the "there" involved is a very special "there," at once a physical destination and a spiritual goal. Thus *darstellen*, a current German verb, usually rendered "represent," clearly indicates that the thing "represented" is made present *there* and nowhere else, *precisely* there, in that "there" which is operationally optimal. So here *darhöhen* indicates more than simply "to raise on high thither"; it evokes the august and celestial terminus of the action, the uniqueness of that "there," in a way equaled in intensity and poignancy by King Lear's expiring cry: "Look on her lips, look *there*."—Translator's note.

to do with more than a pious "lifting" up of the heart. It is important that we realize this and make it clear to the congregation because the eschatological purpose can be served precisely only by a total self-abandonment and surrender to God. The practical effects of this upsurge of self-abandonment are listed in the epistle: "to rise from sleep ... lay aside the works of darkness ... put on the armor of light ... put on the Lord Jesus Christ." And these instructions must not remain merely vague pious phrases. They will probably hit a different nerve in each congregation but one thing must be stressed: our congregations will often scarcely be aware of the fact that they are asleep, that they are not really alert to the implications of Christian living; that they are in darkness, judging terrestrial events and, a fortiori, transcendent reality, only in the dim and murky light of earthbound cognition; that they are entirely enveloped in ephemerality, that they are not really living in Christ.

This total self-abandonment, this complete surrender to Christ can lead to undesirable, even threatening complications at every turn of daily life. But this is exactly what characterizes the eschatological and emboldens us in every situation to expand our horizons beyond the terrestrial event-complex, trusting in Christ, in the power of God, and to score a substantial victory over all enemies, knowing that the promised consummation will not disappoint us.

The Communion verse presents an especially fine interpretation of this eschatological promise: "The Lord, now, will grant us his blessing, to make our land yield its harvest." The autumn harvest of our land is the body of Christ, as formed and present in the womb of the Virgin, in the human community of the Church, and in the eucharistic bread and wine. So do we receive him in the Mass and so through him are we certified and confirmed anew as "body of Christ." We ought to be aware what a blessing descends upon us—the gift of God to mankind is the Son of God!— and what harvest we can yield, we who worship here today as a Christian community *in which* Christ's Advent is ripening against the day when he shall manifest himself in the Church in glory consummated.

The coming of Christ is therefore no mere figment of our longing hearts. It is a full-scale cosmic reality, even though still a hidden reality. And we wait for the day when that reality shall become manifest in the parousia; we wait, not in fear and trembling, but in joyous hope of the full flowering of the grace of God even now germinating within us.

THE COMING OF THE LORD

Advent means arrival, the coming of the Lord. If we would celebrate Advent with the Church, we must first of all seek to understand what it means to say: God comes!

The word "come" can be classed among the most primordial words in the vocabulary of religion. For if religion is a loving and unifying encounter with God, it can only be realized by the coming of God. Unfortunately men often treat the coming of God as they do his loving. They often want, in both cases, to take the second step before the first. They think they must first love God so that God will then love them. Yet St. John says expressly in his first epistle that "love resides, not in our showing any love for God, but in his showing love for us first.... Yes, we must love God; he gave us his love first" (1 Jn 4, 10.19). In just the same way, we cannot come to God unless he has first come to us. This coming of God is not a purely interior mental event; rather it occurs in tangible concrete forms. Thus the coming of God is synonymous in content with the *self-revelation* of God. Therefore anyone who reads and meditates upon Holy Scripture, which is a sign of his continual coming to us, will readily understand that its real content is precisely the proclamation of the coming of God. For what is creation if not the inpouring of divine perfections into nothingness? The express mention of the fact that "darkness hung over the deep; but already, over its waters, stirred the breath of God" is likewise a proclamation of God, as are the commands of God issued into the primordial chaos. Again and again, in the history of the patriarchs, the words of the prophets, the destinies of the chosen people, we encounter a historical advent of God. He comes to individuals, he comes to the whole people, he enters into the Holy of holies of the Ark of the covenant and of the temple. His coming is the clue to history and the fundamental theme of the chosen people of the Old Covenant, whose ultimate reason for existence we know to be the heralding of him who is to come, the Messiah, and the waiting for him. (Incidentally: it would be a very fine Advent exercise for the Christian family or other Christian communities to seek out and trace this coming of God in the history of Israel.) But all of this is only a prelude to that coming of God in which the Word becomes flesh.

All these thoughts are in general quite familiar to us, so familiar that we think that that is the end of the matter. God has come in Jesus Christ, he is with us through this same Christ in his grace through faith and the sacraments; every individual Christian and the Church of Christ as a community are surely signs that God has come and is henceforth forever with us. "And behold I am with you all through the days that are coming, until the consummation of the world," says our Lord at the end of the Gospel according to St. Matthew.

To such an extent do we Christians today live in the belief in the presence of the Lord, preeminently in the holy Eucharist, and so great is our joy at this presence that we almost forget that the same Lord Jesus Christ who lay as a baby in the crib, traversed Palestine as teacher and wonder-worker, died as a victim on the cross, rose again and sent us his Spirit to guide the Church infallibly in the interpretation of his words and actions and to assure us of his very life in the Church, that this same Christ continued to speak right up to the end of his earthly life of his coming, even when he was already there, of a coming that lies beyond the Church and her sacraments.

The New Testament is just as permeated as is the Old with the promise and expectation of a new coming of Christ, despite the fact that he who is to come has already appeared. It is spoken of in the gospels, in the epistles and preeminently in the Apocalypse. This last book of the Bible is so necessary, so downright irreplaceable amid the pandemonium of our days that it is difficult to understand why we in fact leave it almost entirely to the extremist sects and say nothing about it to our Catholic congregations. This last book of the Bible teaches us: "The Spirit and my bride bid me come; let everyone who hears this read out say, Come." The seer tells us the answer of the Lord: "Indeed I am coming soon." And the company of the faithful cry once more: "Come, Lord Jesus!" (Ap 22, 17.20).

Now the question is this: how could such a sincere and passionate longing for the coming of Jesus be possible if everything had already been fulfilled with his Palestinian ministry and with the Church founded by him? Since it obviously could not be possible the next question is whether we Christians today still live in this same vital and poignant longing. And since it is not difficult to demonstrate that we in fact do not, the final question is whether such a Christendom has not become like the old man who is always thinking of how it was "in the good old days" of his childhood and youth, who can talk of nothing else but these ancient memories and in the process wastes the present and, a fortiori, neglects the promise of the future.

If we now, after asking ourselves these questions, turn to a consideration of our Advent rites as they are celebrated in almost total divorce from their liturgical arrangement by families, associations, monasteries and parishes, with very often an exclusive concentration on the coming of Christ in the crib of Bethlehem, an advent that lies more than nineteen hundred years in the past, must we not then feel that we give the impression of a people whose great future is already behind it? There is really no denying the fact that our Advent rites are in general retrospectively oriented. Of course we sing, "O come, O come, Emmanuel," and "O Saviour, bow the heavens and come," but we feel, even as we sing these hymns, that all such cries of longing on the part of the Old Testament chosen people have been entirely fulfilled by the advent of Christ in Bethlehem. These are the songs sung in anxious nights by the people to whom God gave the promise. And when we sing them now, just because it is Advent, then we "think ourselves back" into the days before Christ, pretending that the Messiah has not yet appeared. But this involves a psychological distortion which in the long run can only suit ill our entire spiritual life.

No, the coming of the Lord is truly an event in the future, even for us in our day and for every generation that will come after us. What was begun in Bethlehem is still awaiting *fulfillment*; for what the prophets promised has been fulfilled totally and entirely neither by the Palestinian ministry of Jesus nor yet with his continuing life in the Church. What is still to come is the Kingdom of God in the glory of the returning Christ. For this we keep watch, beyond the calamities of history and the incursions of the demons we await and look forward with passionate longing to this coming of the Lord that will put an end to all this pandemonium and establish the Kingdom of God. To this end will he come and toward this coming, this Advent, is directed the whole of our true longing.

This passionate craving found its expression in the first Christian generations in that mighty petition that stormed the heavens: "Let the figure of this earth pass away and let the glory of the Lord be revealed!"

And we, too, must learn to utter such a cry, still more passionately than did the children of Israel in their day. For we see more clearly than they what that end will be: a share in the dominion of Christ. We see it more clearly because we have known the entire historical event of the life of Jesus. What still unites us to the children of Israel today is the longing for the consummation of the redemption. In this respect, we live in expectation just as do the pious Jews of our age.

The petition "thy kingdom come" in the Lord's own prayer is a profession of this longing and an exercise in this expectation. Would it not be good if we were to pray it in Advent thus meaningfully with full deliberation?

The prayer before meals, "Come, Lord Jesus, be our guest! Let these thy gifts by thee be blest," [1] may well be a modest covert in which this all-inundating longing for the coming of the Lord has found refuge and perpetuation in the wide reaches of popular piety to this day. It is, if I am not mistaken, the only instance of the Christian family in our day still praying for the coming of Christ. How fine it would be if this simple prayer could serve as a catalyst for the great longing for the last coming, the last great advent of the Lord to the unending banquet of the heavenly kingdom. Then our Christian families could celebrate Advent again with genuine piety and the proper disposition, even as the Church herself celebrates it.

"TO MAKE A GOOD ADVENT"

The coming of Christ is not like that of any other. This dawns upon us when we consider that he has already been here upon our earth at a definite point in human history, that he is still here among us and in us in word and sacrament through faith, and that he is still, for all of this, the true and veritable Coming One. This is truly a great mystery: his coming, his advent! It is not to be grasped with human longings or human feelings, however earnest and expectant.

Because the Coming One is one who was once among us and is even now already among us, his coming, his advent, can only be celebrated by those who are already in him and he in them. Not every bride longing for fulfillment understands him and calls him to come to her but rather, "the Spirit and *my* bride," namely the bride who is already filled with his Spirit, his vital breath. Only she can, by his vital power, truly long for him and really call him to her. The voice of the bride who calls in the power of the Spirit cannot be ignored. But this "bride in the

[1] The original of this typically German prayer is: *Komm, Herr Jesus, sei unser Gast, und segne, was Du uns bescheret hast!*—Translator's note.

spirit" is the Church, at once Christ's bride and Christ's body.

Apart from her—we must be quite clear on this point, however strange and even offensive this may sound at first hearing—there is no true Advent celebration, however cozy and picturesque may be the civic and family festivities. Let us put it quite plainly: it is only the Church who stages genuine and effective Advent celebrations, by vitalizing our experience of the coming of the Lord in her mysteries with the proclamation of the word and the celebration of the sacraments and of the Eucharist, leading our minds in this way to the last radiant appearance, in the sense of epiphany, of the Lord.

There is unmistakable testimony, in the unfolding of the revelation that God has given us in the Old and the New Testament, to the fact that the Lord has promised his coming to his people, and to the individual only insofar as he is one of the community of the people of God. Thus we can readily understand why the reference in the Advent liturgy is again and again to the people of Israel, the people of God, Sion, Jerusalem. "The people" is addressed first of all, and all individuals only in function of their membership. And this designation "people of God" now signifies the *new people of God*, the Jerusalem from above, the flock of Jesus Christ, his Church. She alone has been given the promise of the Coming One as a blessing for herself and for all men and for the whole world. For her sake does he come, his advent is meant for her, because he is already united with her, for she is his bride whom he cannot leave behind forsaken. And so the chief sense of his advent is not judgment but rather the blessed nuptial union in the magnificence and power of the Lord of heaven and earth. The judgment passed upon the wicked is the exclusion from this blessed union of those who have declined, with their insipid earthbound excuses, the participation in his nuptials. For such his coming into the world can only be a judgment. But not for that reason does the Lord come; rather he comes to lead his bride, his flock, into his glory.

Let us listen and hear to what a tremendous extent the Church is the central figure in the advent of the Lord and let us note well when such words are borne in upon us in the Advent liturgy. Then we will be compelled to realize that we, the Christian community, the company of the faithful, are signified by these Advent designations.

"From Sion, perfect in beauty, God shines forth. Muster in my presence my faithful servants, who honor my covenant still with sacrifice" (Gradual, second Sunday of Advent). "Jerusalem, right soon shall come thy salvation, why dost thou consume thyself in grief? Is there no counselor at thy side because sorrow hath overcome thee? I will be thy savior and deliverer, fear not, for I am the Lord, thy God, the Holy One of Israel and thy Redeemer" (Responsory after Lesson 1, Matins of Thursday, second week of Advent). "Weep not, O city of Jerusalem, for the Lord hath pity on thee and will take away from thee all tribulation; behold the Lord cometh in power and his arm will have dominion" (Responsory after Lesson 3, Matins of Thursday, second week of Advent). "City of our strength, Sion, the Lord will be to thee wall and bulwark. Open the gates, for the Lord is with us" (second Antiphon, first Vespers of second Sunday of Advent). "People of Sion, behold the Lord shall come to save the nations; and the Lord shall make the glory of his voice to be heard to rejoice your heart" (Introit, second Sunday of Advent). "Rejoice exceedingly, O daughter of Sion; announce it abroad, O daughter of Jerusalem, behold, your king . . . will come to you" (Offertory, Ember Saturday in Winter). "For the law shall come forth from Sion, and the word of the Lord from Jerusalem" (lesson, Ember Wednesday in Winter) "Lift up thine eyes, Jerusalem and look upon the power of the king; behold, the Holy One cometh to free thee from thy fetters." "Upon thee, Jerusalem, the Lord shall dawn, upon thee his splendor shall be revealed" (Is 60, 2). "Even as a mother comforts her children, so will I comfort you, saith the Lord; and out of Jerusalem, my chosen city, shall succor come to you and ye shall see it and your heart shall rejoice. I will pour out salvation upon Sion and my glory upon Jerusalem" (Responsory after Lesson 2, Matins of Friday, second week of Advent).

By virtue of this link between the coming of Christ and his Church, the Advent liturgy goes far behind the purely interior subjective mystical union with Christ. Precisely the passages cited above, stressing on the one hand the coming of the Lord to "his city," to "his kingdom," while implying on the other hand the appropriateness of such titles as "ruler," "king," "prince," "deliverer," "lord of vengeance" (all of them used in the Advent liturgy) for that coming Lord—precisely these passages and these titles show that the coming of the Lord has a political character, involving considerations of civil law. "Political" must not, of course, be understood in this case in the sense of secular politics (national or international); but these ascriptions do show that the Coming One is determined to set the world aright. This is still further underscored by such phrases as: "The scepter of the kingdom will be upon his head. . . . Sion shall be a crown jewel in the hand of her God."

Here, therefore, does not dominate the ineffable intimate sphere of private, individualistic, Christocentric mysticism (the coming of the "Bridegroom of the Soul"); rather the individual is incorporated into the effects and blessing of Christ's coming in the Church and through the Church and by the Church as a member of the people of Christ. The Church here appears as Cardinal Franzelin described her at Vatican I: the conversion of the world into the Kingdom of God. Therefore the liturgy does not say, "Rejoice, beloved soul" but rather, "Arise, O Jerusalem, [people of God], and stand on high [in full public view], and behold the joy that comes to you from your God" (Communion verse, third Sunday of Advent). A "private" Advent rite is just as unthinkable as the so-called "secular" Advent festivities.

This will alienate and disconcert many who will fear that their subjective piety may be handicapped by this sort of Advent rites. Behind this fear lies concealed that misunderstanding which seems nearly ineradicable in many, both of the laity and the clergy, which confuses "subjective" and "personal." There can be no genuine piety, liturgical or paraliturgical, which is not deeply *personal*. But "subjective" means something quite different. Any bias toward subjectivity signifies that the individual is desirous of defending the boundaries of his human individuality, even against the Church and revelation. But surely there must also be Catholics, lay and clerical, who are quite able to thankfully and joyfully accomplish the prescriptions of revelation and of the worshiping Church in such a personal fashion that these liturgical forms become entirely their own personal possession, leading them forth out of the smallness and narrowness of human thinking and feeling, human desires and human longings into the vast infinite reaches of divine reality. Such a meaningful and by no means depersonalizing exodus occurs every time that a Christian interpolates himself in personal concelebration with the Church into the *opus Christi*, including the mystery of his Advent. Those who so jealously guard their "subjective piety" might well be reminded of the word of the Lord: "He who loves his life shall lose it; but he who hates it, shall gain it." Why is it that we often do not trust our congregation's capacity to achieve a personal participation in the official worship of the Church? Why is there so often a mania for psychological substitutes which void entirely the most precious aspects? What characterizes the official worship of the *sponsa Christi* and exalts it above all subjective opinions and expectations is the simple fact that the Church as Christ's bride who awaits him can present the coming of Christ in her rites with that sureness of touch which is proper to her alone, because the Lord is hers in a special way. And therefore it is the Church in her liturgy who comprehends and proclaims the whole immeasurable scope of the coming of Christ, over against which proclamation the individual presents a cramped and sorry figure, caught in the toils of his own personal subjective fads. Only he who has experienced this unbounded majesty, grandeur, and elation of the coming of Christ as celebrated by the Church is in a position to judge what is being missed by those who deny themselves this experience. And it is not enough to have experienced it but once: the experience and impression must be reinforced by annually repeated meditation and concelebration.

Those, therefore, who wait upon the Lord and keep watch against his coming with and in the Church acquire in that Church the conviction and the certitude of the triumphal coming of Christ, even in the face of personal failures and afflictions or the chaotically confused world situation which might humanly depress them or reduce them to despair. But the conviction and the certitude are not the only advantages of such an identification with the mind of the Church; this identification also channels all our expectations and longings beyond all human and earthly dimensions to the fullness of God. And these longings and expectations are heightened still further by the promises of the Lord who is coming to his bride, to his people!

CHAPTER 49

Second Sunday of Advent

"BLESSED IS HE WHO IS
NOT SCANDALIZED IN ME"

The short sentence with which this Sunday's gospel begins describes a situation whose full tragedy is not immediately obvious: "John had heard in prison of the works of Christ." Now this John was the man who had proclaimed Jesus before the people to be the Lamb of God, who had openly and publicly certified him as the Messiah, who had learned directly of his power and greatness by divine revelations. Now this same John is languishing in prison and the *greater than I* whom he had proclaimed, this Jesus, is walking about in Palestine preaching and working the occasional miracle, without lifting a finger to free from prison the very man who had initiated him into this messianic activity. And he would have the power to do this, were he the promised redeemer. And it would surely be his responsibility, thinks John, recalling what he has so often heard from his father Zacharias about the redeemer who would "deliver us from the hands of all our enemies."

John cannot understand the inaction of Jesus. That he should do nothing whatever to lead his own to the freedom of the people of God but rather lets them languish thus behind prison walls! Not that John doubts, but he simply cannot understand anything about the situation any more: everything has developed so entirely differently than he had expected and preached. Was it perhaps after all going to be necessary to wait for another?

He who is to come realizes the external affliction and the interior distress of his precursor. He takes note of John's question but promises no relief. His answer, brief enough in all conscience, ends with a beatitude, not "blessed is he who comes out of prison" but rather "blessed is he who is not scandalized in me." So Jesus admits the possibility of a scandal occasioned by himself but he is by no means ready to remove that scandal. The Baptist must go through the scandal, not around it. And so must we!

Or can it be that the advent of Christ, in which we believe, in which indeed we live, is without scandal for us? Would we not like to see many things, a great many things, different than they are? Not in the least from motives of personal advantage but precisely in the interest of him "who is to come" himself? Do we not wish that he were better preached and better understood? That his compassion and justice were more readily discernible in the field of social and economic relations and his power and glory in the field of political life? Every single one of us who is not a thoughtless fellow-traveler on the latest bandwagon has his own special disappointment to bear. Which is yours, fellow-Christian? Identify it and then apply to your own situation that word of Christ, "blessed is he who is not scandalized in me."

"Whatever things have been written have been written for our instruction." So begins the epistle. And it prepares us for the story of John the Baptist as related in the gospel, so that his distress will not take us unawares. And we are further told that "Christ has received you to the honor of God." This is our reality! Whatever may happen, however much our plans and wishes may be thwarted it is in this Christ—in him alone and in no other—that the faithfulness and compassion of God operate, in that he has "received" us who came from among the gentile peoples. He was not bound to do so by any promise he had made; but he has assimilated us to the promises made to his own people.

And because God is faithful and merciful, we are told, with

respect to the scandals that are bound up with the Advent of the Lord: "Now may the God of hope fill you with all joy and peace in believing, and may you abound in hope and in the power of the Holy Spirit."

These express words with which the epistle ends are a confirmation by the apostle of what was said to us already in the Introit, in which we are addressed as the "people of Sion." The Lord will come to save the gentiles (the nations—all nations of the earth) and we shall hear the voice of his glory in the joy of our heart. Similar promises recur in the Gradual verses following the epistle, always referring to "Sion" and "the house of the Lord," names applicable to every Christian congregation. We repeat them as a prayer when we present our offerings and hear them anew as a wonderful reassurance even as we receive the body of the Lord: "Jerusalem [here again, it is we who are summoned] arise, and stand on high, and behold the joy that comes to you from your God!"

This is the reality that hovers around us in the coming of the Lord. The scandals remain but the joy of the Lord protects us from bitterness. We are rather accorded that serenity which is proper to the divine beatitude itself, if only we are "not scandalized in him."

CHAPTER 50

Third Sunday of Advent

ADVENT PROMISES

Expectation and longing can be kindled either by subjective dreams and wishes or by objective promises. The Advent rites of the Church rest exclusively upon objective promises, exclusively because we would never even be able to conceive on our own, by our own power, the expectations of the Advent season. And this objective promise of Advent is characterized not only by the nobility and grandeur of the salvific blessings in prospect but also and especially by the certainty with which these blessings are assured us. Both the grandeur of vision and the certainty of attainment would be impossible to our purely subjective longing stemming from human cravings alone.

So the promises of God are what stimulate our longing again and again to aim at things divine and not merely at things human. The time to exercise ourselves in such longing is the Advent season, for in that season the Church is to a greater and more intense degree than at any other time the waiting Church, the Church of bridal longing, uttering the cry put into her heart by the Spirit, "Come, Lord Jesus!"

The question now arises: what does modern Christendom know of the promises of God and of his Messiah, and to what extent does Christendom still live in and from these promises? To the question as to what are the promises of Our Lady of Fatima or what those of the Sacred Heart to St. Margaret Mary Alacoque, a great many persons will be able to give an exact answer forthwith. But if we—and this means every single reader of these lines—ask ourselves what God has promised us through Christ, honestly now, which of us would be able to give an immediate and unhesitating answer? Most of us certainly would be able quickly to muster general phrases like "get to heaven," "attain beatitude," "eternal life"; many would also say "see God," or "resurrection from the dead." These answers are all, of course, quite correct, but really these phrases are timeworn like coins that have passed from hand to hand and are scarcely given a second attentive glance. Certainly if God had said nothing else through his prophets and through his Christ, then we should have to be satisfied with these promises. But granting for a moment that he had said something else, something more, that he had spoken more plainly about his designs for us and our world, in that case ought we not to be more concerned to know just what he had said? And if we never did it at any other time, would it not be a very fine and necessary assignment for the Advent season to search the Scriptures to find what exactly God has promised us outright? There are so many favorite popular "Advent exercises" which are quite superficial; *this one* would introduce us to an immeasurably magnificent vision and teach us to cry with the passionate longing of the bride, "Come, Lord Jesus!"

The promises were made to the fathers, the patriarchs, and again and again clearly proclaimed to the people by the prophets. All of these promises had in substance but one single theme: *the promised land* in which the Messiah would unfurl the ensign of his dominion, by the power of which he would unite all lands, their kings and their peoples, into an absolute ecumene. So, too, is his picture shown to us in the Advent season: "King of kings and Lord of lords," "He shall have dominion from sea unto sea and from the river to the ends of the earth." (We ought to make a special effort during the Advent season to keep this picture of him "who is to come" in the dominant foreground of our religious practices and meditations.) The dominion that he establishes is the royal dominion of God, the kingdom of God, not somewhere up in the air but permeating the whole of created nature.

The Israel of the Old Covenant lived on this longing for the *promised land;* Israel really lived on this longing, did not merely dream of it! In times when the national and religious existence of the people seemed doomed to extinction (during the Babylonian captivity, or the wars of the Machabees), Israel held out in the strength of this very concrete longing. Israel remained, even in captivity and bondage, what it had always been: the chosen and free people of God. And this same staying power can be observed even today among pious Jews; its roots lie not in any political or racial considerations but rather in the longing for the kingdom, for the fulfillment of the promises made to the fathers. And so in effect it was not the people that supported and supports the kingdom, but rather the longing for the kingdom which supported and sustained the people of the Old Testament and supports and sustains the people of the New, as well.

In the days of Jesus, likewise, there was in substance but one religious motif: the kingdom. Think of Nicodemus; think of the Beatitudes in the Sermon on the Mount, with their promises of the "kingdom of heaven" and "the land" (Mt 5, 5); think of the constant questions of the disciples, the last petition of the dying thief. Unless I am mistaken, the "kingdom of heaven," the "kingdom of God," the "promised land," have pretty well disappeared from the current religious vocabulary of our time. Perhaps the reason is that kingship and the very idea of empire have been so discredited in our day. Another reason may well be that such notions seem to us too ponderous and materialistic to be fitted into our "purified" and "spiritualized" devotion and piety. We are always hearing about the "material" and "political" corruptions of the messianic hope of the ancient Jews. However this may be,

such dangers did not impel either Jesus or his disciples to strike
the term or the theme of "the kingdom" from their preaching. The
kingdom stands at the inception of the preaching of Jesus and at
the end of the preaching of the apostles. And throughout it has
the sense of a reality of our own world.

The Church's Advent message is entirely in line with the message of Jesus and the apostles: it is equally a message of the
kingdom. Of course the kingdom here portrayed to us is not an
earthly paradise pandering to the desires of the senses, as it seems
to be, for instance, in the progress theories of the politicians with
an exclusive this-worldly bent. But on the other hand, the kingdom and the land promised to the people of God certainly cannot
be considered a purely spiritual abstract notion, a pure idea with
no real value for our world. The promised land is still a "land"
even if it is a "renewal of the face of the earth," a "new heaven
and a new earth," even as the kingdom of God is to be inhabited
not by astral men but by historical mankind, by us, who will be
conformed to the glory of the risen body of Christ (cf. Phil 3, 21).
Whether it is a question therefore of the "land" or of its human
inhabitants, it is only the "form and fashion" which will "pass
away" (cf. 1 Cor 7, 31). Our world will remain in substance,
even if its new state and composition are presently incomprehensible to us. Ever since the Logos has truly been "made flesh" and
the "spirit of the Lord has filled the whole earth"—not some
imaginary world but our own cosmos!—there is indeed in the
realm of the human the paradox of a "spiritual body" (1 Cor
15, 44), but there is no such phenomenon as "pure spirituality."
The world remains a world (Rom 8, 20 f.) even though irradiated
and transformed by the glory of God and the Lamb (Ap 21, 23).
Thus the "Kingdom of God" is not a geographical or astronomical
realm among others, it is not for instance above or to one side of
our world, it *is* our world, newly constituted by God's glory.

In this sense must we understand the Advent promises. They
are promises of the peace, harmony, fullness, and beauty tran-

scending all natural imagination, which creation will attain in the coming of the Lord.

"On that day the mountains shall drop down sweetness and the hills flow with milk and honey." "The fields of the desert places of Israel are fragrant with green shoots, for behold, our God cometh in his power and his brightness is all about him." "Thrills the barren desert with rejoicing; the wilderness takes heart and blossoms, fair as the lily. Blossom on blossom, it will rejoice and sing for joy; all the majesty of Lebanon is bestowed on it, all the grace of Carmel and of Saron ... Springs will gush out in the wilderness, streams flow through the desert; ground that was dried up will give place to pools, barren land to wells of clear water; where the serpent had its lair once, reed and bulrush will show their green. A high road will stretch across it, by divine proclamation kept holy ..." (second reading, Ember Saturday in Winter).

Faced with such imaginative descriptions, we must not ask, Can such things be? Rather we must relearn this language. These descriptions are not the fine frenzy of poetic exaggeration but rather the attempt to portray in human language and images the new indescribable cosmic reality, radically indescribable for us in this present age because the words and the corresponding visual references of those words are still hidden from us. The imaginative descriptions are therefore in no sense exaggerations. On the contrary, they lag far behind that reality which will be the overt epiphany of our world as "the promised land," "the kingdom of God"—a reality at which the angels rejoice already: "Heaven and earth are full of thy glory."

This exclamation of wonder refers to created nature apart from man, of whom still greater things are predicted. The promises of Christ in his parables speak of the Lord setting his faithful servant over all his possessions, of the beatitude of the marriage feast, and so forth. And how few are aware of the further promises made by the Lord in his glory to "him who overcometh": "I will give him authority over the nations; to herd them like sheep with a crook of iron ... and the star of morning shall be his." [1] "Who wins the victory? I will let him share my *throne* with me; I too have won the victory, and now I sit sharing my Father's throne" (Ap 2, 26 f.; 3, 21).

And in all of these promises, it is *we* who are meant. Do we realize that in these days? Do we take this unimaginable exaltation really seriously any more? For precisely such is the picture painted for us of our world and of ourselves in the promises of Christ! To savor these promises, to fill heart and mind with them, to make them our vital motive force: this is the assignment of the Advent season. Otherwise we shall never learn to cry as passionately as does the Church: "Come, Lord Jesus!"

The guarantor that this longing will not "delude us" (Rom 5, 5,) is he of whom the gospel on the third Sunday of Advent says that he is among us and we know him not. We do not know him because his presence among us in word and sacrament, even in the visible community of the Church, is still a hidden presence. We talk about him a great deal but we do not know him. Did we but know him in his power and glory, in his beatitude and that fullness of life which even now he dispenses among us and in us, then would our longing know no bounds, the longing not only to possess him in faith but even to gaze upon and enjoy his presence immediate and entire: "Let the figure of this earth pass away and let the glory of the Lord be revealed in it and in us!" Such is the longing of the royal bride for the kingdom.

Fiat! fiat! "So be it! so be it!" To this cry we are impelled by "the promise of the land" and by our longing that transcends all human desires.

---

[1] Pinsk does not comment further on this promise, but if we refer it, as does Msgr. Knox, to Ap 22, 16, where "I, Jesus" calls *himself* "the bright star that brings in the day," then this promise becomes the most prodigious of all, implying more even than a share in Christ's dominion, more even than the intimate union promised in the high–priestly prayer ("one in us, as thou Father, art in me, and I in thee"—Jn 17, 21). For such a promise evokes in the order of a divine *promise*, that most staggering of all gospel paradoxes enunciated in parable form in Lk 12, 37.—Translator's note.

ADVENT JOY

Anyone prompted by the violet vestments and the suppression of the Gloria to think of Advent as a season of sorrowful penance would certainly regard the third Sunday of Advent, with its insistent cry of *Gaudete*, "Rejoice," as a foreign element. But a reflection in depth on the preceding Sundays has already shown us that joy is not foreign to Advent. On this Sunday, Advent joy is the overt theme. Introit and epistle speak of it in identical words and both know but one ground for that joy: "The Lord is near."

It may seem pedantic to analyze this simple sentence; but such an analysis is mandatory if it is to be thoroughly understood, not merely theoretically and intellectually, but in such a way that we can, by a real act of will, make it our own interior possession. Let us therefore attempt the analysis. The proximity of the Lord can only be a ground for joy if he is himself joy. Now there are plenty of pietistically colored hymns in which we sing of "Jesus, my joy"—but in this Mass the stake is higher.

In the farewell discourses, Jesus twice spoke expressly of *his* joy (Jn 15, 11; 17, 13). This joy of his is therefore something special, different from the "joy of the world." It may even indeed seem to be sadness and sorrow in the context of the world, because it has no connection whatever with the joy of the world, indeed standing in contrast with that joy (Jn 16, 20–22). This must be carefully considered in any decision as to whether Jesus of Nazareth is really "my joy" or not. For the company of the faithful gathered together in the word of Christ and united around his altar, there is no other ground for joy except only him. Otherwise this Sunday's Mass is rendered impossible of meaningful participation.

But what, then, is the joy of the Lord, his own personal joy? I believe it is the joy of his human nature at its union with the Son of God, a union filling his human body and his human soul "bodily" with the whole fullness of God. In this joy, the "Son of man" goes through suffering and death and enters into the glory of the Father.

It must be admitted that such joy is far from self-evident for us. Our joy seeks in the first instance other objects within this world of ours. Hence Paul's insistent admonition in the epistle that we should "rejoice in the Lord." Hence, too, his subsequent allusion to the need for poise and imperturbability, for overcoming "anxiety." Poise and imperturbability are essential in the face of the perturbing assaults of the world. But how can we remain so imperturbable? Not by resignation or clenched-teeth endurance because we can "do nothing about it anyway"; rather our imperturbability must derive from the wealth of that blessedness that we have in the Lord who remains throughout the deepest joy of our being.

Herein does the great and crucial principle of the Christian posture become evident: not the compulsion to renunciation because of incapacity or defect, but rather the ability to renounce the ephemeral because we possess the eternal, with which we are invested by the nearness of the Lord. From this abundant possession comes the peace that guards our hearts and our minds and makes them strong. If we acknowledge this, then is the Lord in very truth our joy and then will his nearness heighten our joy unceasingly unto the superabundance of the riches of God. His nearness? Do we really feel that nearness? Or do we not rather stand uncomprehending like the priests and levites before the Baptist who tells them, "In the midst of you there has stood one whom you do not know"? Two things are therefore demanded of us by the Pauline admonition to joy: that we *realize* and that we *affirm* that he is really near to us. We shall not succeed in fulfilling these demands without constant practice. Thus, for example, when we can find no cause for joy whatever in some situation, when vexation upon vexation breaks over our head, *then* let us triumphantly proclaim: Christ is my joy, because in him I am partaker of "the one supreme Godhead." I need not wait for this apotheosis until the last day, for even now he is near to me in faith, in his word, in his sacrament, in the community of his Church.

Such an exercise in recognition and affirmation is the whole sense of this Sunday's epistle. Such an exercise is called for by the word of the Baptist, "In the midst of you there has stood one whom you do not know." Such an exercise we attempt to perform with the declaration of the trust implicit in the petitions of the Gradual. Such an exercise we again attempt in the affirmation of the Offertory, "O Lord, you have blessed your land; you have restored Jacob from captivity; you have forgiven the sinfulness of your people." (For, be it well noted, none of this is true nor is our affirmation honest if we speak from the purely human point of view: none of these statements can be honestly made without the exercise of faith.) Such an exercise we essay a final time when we have received the body of the Lord. There we are summoned in the Communion verse, as members of the Lord "who is to come," to proclaim his joy to the fainthearted and the wavering.

We who carry within us the joy of Christ are to become in that same Christ instruments to help the world achieve happiness. So did Paul regard his ministry to the community (2 Cor 1, 24) and so must the Church also, if she be truly apostolic, regard her ministry to mankind. Then and then only will the Pauline admonition be fulfilled: "Rejoice in the Lord ... the Lord is near." *Therefore* "rejoice in the Lord." The practice of such recognition, affirmation and rejoicing is a part of the preparation for the coming Lord.

CHAPTER 51

Fourth Sunday of Advent

"ALL MANKIND SHALL SEE THE SALVATION OF GOD"

The day of the second coming of Christ as the day of judgment is for most of us a day of fear and trepidation. This may be the reason for our inability to make much of it, for its being in our life as Christians a motive for consternation and apprehension, whereas the apostolic and primitive Christian community longed above all else to see that day. For St. Paul likewise this day is an ardently awaited consolation for it will bring with it the justification of his apostolic ministry. The words proclaimed to us today from his first letter to the Corinthians are the words of a man keenly aware of his apostolic office and serenely sovereign in his exercise of that office. The apostle is the "steward of the mysteries of God." For such a one the sole duty is to be faithful in his stewardship, in the administration of these mysteries. He will therefore have to ask himself again and again if he has unreservedly transmitted to his congregation the fullness of the treasures entrusted to the Church by revelation, or whether he has devoted himself to his own favorite topics and thereby neglected the great wealth of revelation. Do we today preach the theological content of the Old Covenant? Is it not an intolerable state of affairs when priests, both of the older and the younger generation, claim that the Psalms have nothing to say to the modern world, that they are a Jewish product and should be replaced where possible by

modern prayers? What are we doing to project that image of
Christ which transcends the synoptic gospels, say the cosmic image
of Christ according to Ephesians and Colossians, or the *political*
image (Colossians and Apocalypse)? What are we doing to preach
Christian eschatology? Eschatology with all its implications is the
official theme set by the Church for the period from the eighteenth
Sunday after Pentecost right through the Advent season. Can the
commissioned cleric who suppresses all of this still call himself a
faithful minister of the mysteries of God?

Paul could, with a good conscience, call himself such a faithful
minister, hence his superb unconcern and serenity in the face of
any human judgment: "Yet for myself I make little account of
your scrutiny, or of any human audit-day; I am not even at pains
to scrutinize my own conduct ... it is the Lord's scrutiny I must
undergo." Is this not the expression of a splendid trust in the day
of Christ? And Paul wants us to have the same trusting confidence: "You do ill, therefore, to pass judgment prematurely, before the Lord's coming; he will bring to light what is hidden in
darkness, and reveal the secrets of men's hearts; then each of us
will receive his due award from God." And this last sentence we
find confirmed once again at the end of the gospel. We are commissioned to make ready in the desert the highway of the Lord;
this is no easy or pleasant assignment but in the end "all mankind
shall see the salvation of God."

Such is the last day: it brings salvation, peace, order, and justice. If we learn to see it in this light, then we shall no longer
understand the Old Testament cry: "Let the clouds rain down the
just one!" as implying for us merely a reversion to a point in the
history of the as yet unredeemed Jewish people, to the songs they
sang in anxious nights. Rather shall we feel how poignantly applicable this cry is to our own situation, how much we should yearn
for the manifestation of the Just One and Saviour.

For this first time in the Advent Sunday Masses, there is
reference in today's Mass to *Mary* (Offertory and Communion
verse). But even these texts point beyond the event of the birth

in Bethlehem, inasmuch as the Church, who carries on the function of the Mother of Christ, makes them her own. The community of Christian worshipers here assembled on this Sunday is functioning as Virgin mother of the mystical Christ, carrying the historical event toward its final consummation, when the process of the coming of Christ, begun in the incarnation, will attain its glorious denouement in the second coming of the Lord.

The texts of the Gradual put into our mouths the right words with which to go out, as a Church, to meet the coming Lord, as he approaches us step by step in each succeeding liturgy.

THE EFFICACIOUS SANCTIFYING RITE OF THE CHURCH

"The King, the coming Lord—come, let us do homage to him!" These are the initial words of the hours of the Breviary during the first two weeks of Advent. On the third Sunday of Advent and the days following, the invitation becomes more urgent: "Now is the Lord already near—come, let us do homage to him!" On December 21, the Antiphon to the *Benedictus* runs: "Fear ye not, for on the fifth day our Lord will come to you!" And on the day before the vigil of Christmas this same Antiphon runs: "Behold, all things have been fulfilled which were spoken by the angel of the Virgin Mary." On the vigil day itself, the whole of the Church's praying, in an atmosphere of supreme tension, takes on the coloring of "today" and "tomorrow": "Today you shall know that the Lord is coming; and tomorrow you shall see his glory." "On the morrow will be taken away the iniquity of the earth." "Tomorrow shall be to you salvation." Such are the recurrent themes of the Vigil Office. But even throughout the whole course of the Advent season, the Church has been adjuring the heavens and the earth in most urgent terms to give us the Lord: "Drop down dew, you heavens, from above, and let the clouds rain down the just one. Let the earth be opened and bud forth a savior." And the Lord himself is constantly being implored: "Come, Lord

and tarry no longer." And at the point at which the longing
threatens to become exasperation, we are promised: "The Lord
will come and will not delay."

An intelligent adult must ask what is behind all this constant
and unremitting rekindling of longing, this persistent encouragement to count the very days that separate us from the expected
event. Is it nothing but pious stage props, set up only to be taken
down again without any vestige of that great event occurring to
which our longing has been directed day after day? Were this the
case, there would certainly be no reason to become so involved,
to enter so deeply into this state of longing! For there is no point
in concentrating eager expectation on a certain definite deadline
when it is clear in advance that nothing is going to happen at
the deadline set. The entire procedure would then be nothing but
a playful and irresponsible psychological experiment.

I must confess that I cannot believe that the Church, a fortiori
the praying Church, would be capable of such inanity. The praying Church especially must be taken very seriously indeed. But
what, in that case, *is* the point? What is the Advent-given answer
to our Advent-kindled longing? Does our so passionate longing
encounter an appropriate answer or not?

The satisfying answer is guaranteed us and given us by the
Church, inasmuch as she is *the continuation of the incarnation.*
We are indeed members of Christ, in true and living union with
him who is our head. In the succession of the Christian generations, in which the people of God is perfected, Christ is therefore
moving through the history of our race. The Church is thus the
concrete epiphany, the mystical embodiment of the exalted Lord
in a visible community for the time intervening between his resurrection and his second coming. This Lord Jesus Christ, who lives
and works in us, proceeds with us and in us and through us
toward his second coming that will manifest him before the whole
world. This second coming is therefore being infallibly brought
closer by Christ's own power.

The incarnate Son of God did indeed accept the lowliness of

his earthly human nature in obedience to the Father; but he has
by no means become resigned to it. This comes out clearly in his
prayer to the Father: "Father . . . give glory now to thy Son . . .
now, Father, do thou exalt me at thy own side, in that glory
which I had with thee before the world began" (Jn 17, 1–5).
The same thing is true also for the body which he has assumed
in the visible community of the Church. Christ, the head of this
Church, is by no means simply resigned to the frailties and de-
ficiencies that cling to the visible Church through all generations
to the end of time. Just as he aspired and laid claim for his physical body to the glory which he had with the Father as consub-
stantial Son before the world began, in exactly the same way does
he aspire and lay claim to the same glory for the mystical members of his body, for the community of his Church: "And I have
given them the privilege which thou (Father) gavest to me. . . .
This, Father, is my desire, that all those whom thou hast entrusted
to me may be with me where I am, so as to see my glory, thy
gift made to me, in that love which thou didst bestow upon
me before the foundation of the world" (Jn 17, 22–24).

The destiny of Christ, the clothing of his lowly human nature
in the divine glory, is our destiny as well. Inseparable from his
glorious coming is the glory of his community, the members of
his mystical body.

It is this Christ therefore who leads the humanity of his Church
generation after generation ever nearer to his second coming. His
longing fills the Church and becomes her longing, a longing that
presses on toward the goal of the deification of humanity by the
grace of God.

In another manner but with the same efficacious power has the
Messiah moved through and with the human generations from
the beginning, as witnessed by the genealogies of Jesus in the
gospels of Matthew (1, 1–16) and Luke (3, 23–38).

From generation to generation, he, the promised one, is borne
in the human race; irresistibly do the generations thrust toward
his coming, so that every succeeding generation is nearer to that

coming than was its predecessor. This historical process cannot, to be sure, be established a priori but it is nonetheless a real process in history. So, too, is Christ's coming in our day interpolated into the succession of the generations, no longer according to the flesh but rather in the power of his new life (Spirit); it is inseparably bound to the visible Church, visible in her human members and her actions. And so the words of the apostle in the epistle for the first Sunday of Advent acquire a very real meaning for each and every generation of the New Testament people of God: "...now our salvation is nearer than when we came to believe." Day by day, Christ approaches, in us and with us, more closely to his second coming and therewith to "the promised land." And so we can say today: Tomorrow the Saviour comes nearer to us, the Lord who is hidden within us approaches more closely to the manifestation of his glory. The grace of that coming is therefore an uninterrupted grace, constantly filling and perfecting us.

In the framework of this uninterrupted process, the liturgical rites of the Church have their special importance. This is comparatively easy for the faithful Christian to grasp in the case of the sacraments. Every sacrament advances the coming of Christ not only because of the purely mechanical contraction, during the time consumed by its administration, of the span separating us from his coming, but also because *this present time* is being filled, in the grace of the sacrament, with a *content* related and *deliberately referred* to that state in which God will in very truth "be all in all." Only in that still future state will the capacity of the world and of the human race in that world be filled to the very brim. Now this *"full*-filling" is accomplished (in a hidden and mysterious fashion, to be sure, which can only be grasped by faith) in the program of the Church preeminently in her liturgical rites, which are not limited to the administration of the sacraments but comprehend the celebration of the feasts as well. This liturgical fulfillment naturally occurs also in the season in which the coming of the Lord is portrayed in the celebration of his birth and his epiphany. And so we do in fact experience during Advent a heightening of our implication in the coming of the Lord, and the feast of his birth does in fact fill us with the glory of his coming, for which Advent has prepared our mind and our heart by an increase of knowledge and an intensification of longing. On occasion this is clearly expressed in the prayers of the Mass: "May we receive your mercies, O Lord ... so that we anticipate with due honor the coming feast of our redemption" (Postcommunion, first Sunday of Advent).

Even as the *opus Christi* and his coming is being fulfilled in us who are his body, so also is that which was begun in Mary being fulfilled in us who, as Church, are bride of Christ and mother of the sons of God. This realization imparts to the references to the Virgin mother of the Lord in the Advent liturgy their concrete and vital significance for us. In the worshiping community of Christians solemnizing the incarnation of the Lord, there is being fulfilled again, albeit in a different fashion, what was "spoken by the angel of the Virgin Mary."

And so the *progressive fulfillment* with the glory of the coming Lord is the grace mediated to us by the Advent rites. This is expressed most poignantly in a prayer of the Mozarabic Liturgy:

> We do not pray that thy birth according to the flesh shall be renewed as it once occurred upon this day. Rather do we pray that thy invisible Godhead may be grafted into us.
> May that which was then accorded after the flesh to Mary alone now be granted in the spirit to the Church: that faith unquestioning may conceive thee, the spirit free of all corruption may bear thee, the soul overshadowed by the power of the Most High may quicken with thee evermore.
> Go not forth from us, spring forth rather from within us.

In this sense the Church's liturgy is an efficacious rite, and only as such is it a "sanctifying rite." In this light does this phrase, so often sapped of its true sense by meaningless conventional repetition, acquire again its ancient grandeur and persuade us that it is indeed a rewarding discipline to celebrate with the Church the coming of Christ.

"A HIGHWAY FOR OUR GOD"

St. Luke in his gospel links the preaching of John the Baptist with a purely prophetic message proclaimed more than five hundred years earlier, announcing to the chosen people the end of the Babylonian captivity: "Voice of a herald: 'Clear a road for Yahweh! Lay it through the wasteland! Level in the desert a highway for our God! Fill in every valley! Level hills and mountains! Straighten out the windings, make the rough patches smooth! Yahweh's glory shall shine forth and all mankind shall see it! It is his own decree!'" (Is 40, 53ff.)

This much more literal rendering of the Hebrew idiom makes the familiar translation seem somewhat flat, especially when moralistically inclined preachers proceed to apply its phrases one-sidedly in a "purely spiritual" fashion to the eradication of sin and the practice of virtue. This robs the prophet's words of their primordial monumental grandeur.

For the road here spoken of must not be taken merely figuratively. No, the prophet has in mind actual roadbuilding over impassable terrain, the building of a triumphal procession route such as were laid down for the great monarchs of the East on the occasion of their journeys from their capital to their provinces.

But the prophet's message goes far beyond this. He does indeed retain the picture of the oriental royal progresses, but only to serve as a graphic representation of the road of Yahweh, the highway of God, along which he will march at the head of his people, when he leads them out of bondage into the holy city, Jerusalem. On this great march, he will manifest his power before the face of the peoples and all mankind shall see it. It will be as it was about seven hundred years before, when he marched before his people during the exodus out of Egypt, in the pillar of clouds by day and the pillar of fire by night, to lead them into his land.

Such are the highways of God. They lead out of the bondage of the powers of this world into the freedom of the sons of God. Moses traveled this road with the people about 1200 B.C. out of Egypt toward Canaan; Israel traveled this road about 536 B.C.

from Babylon through the wilderness of the holy Sion. When John the Baptist appears, the people have already long since settled down in their own land and the message of the Baptist is again a call to a triumphal exodus with God along God's highway into the true and definitive kingdom of the messianic age.

This is the highway of Advent. On it God does not cease to meet his people and on it his people marches toward the revelation of salvation. God actually accomplishes this progress through the world and through history in his Church. And the Church's business on this road is stated in the epistle: she administers the mysteries of God. Nothing else! And what is demanded of each and every member—according to the nature of his vocation and commission—is that he "be found trustworthy." This is demanded of *everyone*, since all are ministers of the one royal priesthood of the New Covenant, albeit in various ways and with differing powers. But every single member of the Church will have to answer for the degree of his faithfulness in the communication of the knowledge and wisdom, power and beatitude of life entrusted by God to his Church. This is clearly a grave question for the whole of the Church, for the teachers and the hearers of her message, for those who are ministers of the hierarchical priesthood and those who are members of the universal priesthood.

Do we not so often substitute our own personal thoughts and sentiments, our subjective opinions and experiences for the real divine communication accorded us in revelation? And the danger is always present, what with the limitations of human comprehension, that things private and peripheral will trammel the essential substance. But if we are really faithful in the administration of the mysteries of God, then men can say what they will about us and do what they will against us. We will have no fear "of any human audit-day," for the Lord will be our judge!

One phrase in the Collect acquires specially concrete significance for this triumphal progress over the highway of God. Our sins shackle and impede (*praepediunt*) our feet, so that we cannot march forward; but the Lord looses our fetters. And we besiege him with the insistent plea that he delay not to free his people from their evil deeds. The Gradual tells us that "the Lord is near to all who call upon him," and in that comforting certainty we can wait reassured until he come to bring to light what is hidden in darkness and reveal the secrets of men's hearts, even as the epistle has told us that he will.

So do we travel, in prayer and thanksgiving, in possession and yet in expectation, the highway of our Lord. The fact that there is such a highway in this our day and this our world—that is the glad tidings of this Sunday. Can we be sure of it? Yes, for our pledge is the body of the Lord, filling his Church and making her fruitful, so that the Virgin mother, the Church, conceives and brings forth the sons of God, and so becomes *Emmanuel*, "God with us"!

CHAPTER 52

Christmas

FIRST MASS

The images evoked by the words "nativity" and "epiphany" are entirely in line with the notion of the coming of Christ. And so the season embracing these feasts is the fulfillment of what has been heralded and promised in Advent. The texts from the Breviary for this season are notable for their frequent repetition in the present tense of what was said during Advent in the future tense. A thoughtful meditation on this change of tense reveals the very pace of the Church in the forward movement of the cycle of her year.

A matter of capital importance, theoretically and of course practically as well, for the Christmas sermon, is the maintenance of a sharp distinction between the preaching at Mass and the more affective tones of the crib devotion address. Crib devotions are in the main limited to a poignant evocation of what happened long ago in Bethlehem. Imagination, poetry and sentiment are here quite in place; but not when preaching at Mass. If anyone asks *why* not, the answer is clear: because the Church, in introducing the birth of Christ into the rite of the eucharistic mystery, is opening up before us quite different spiritual vistas than those proffered by carols and crib devotions. Now I quite agree that it would be mulish and pigheaded to try to suppress the emotional elements of the crib devotions *during these devotions themselves*, out of a misplaced enthusiasm for the monumental significance of the incarnation of the Son of God. But it seems to me just as faddish and birdbrained and really retrograde to insist on expatiating *at Mass as well* on nothing but the "holy infant so tender and mild," on the dear little Christ Child and all the chubby little cherubs, when the Church herself is setting an entirely different tone! The proper tone of the Christmas Mass is set by the Church's treatment of the birth of Christ: she does not confine her treatment to the narrow historical limits of the Bethlehem nativity. Rather she reveals to the congregation at worship the *universal* significance of the incarnation as an event which decides the fate of the entire *cosmos*. It is surely high time, therefore, to make an end to the habit of speaking of Christmas as the children's feast par excellence and of acting as if the essential prerequisite of the Christmas spirit were a regress into the golden age of childhood. Christmas is *not* the children's feast; it is the feast on which the adult Christian has to decide anew between the purely interior world of his own fancies and the great objective reality of God in the world.

Now we must substantiate all these contentions by an examination of the texts of the Christmas Masses, whereby it should also be noted that anyone preaching at all three Masses should certainly gear each sermon to the particular texts of the individual Mass.

The historical fact of the birth of Jesus in Bethlehem is reported only in the gospels of the first two Masses. The elements of these historical reports are of no further significance for the structuring of the three Masses. Not even Mary and Joseph are mentioned except in the gospels of the first and second Masses, even though the Station Church of the first and the third Mass (*Statio ad S. Mariam maiorem ad Praesepe* and *ad S. Mariam maiorem*) might have been expected to direct the attention of the worshipers to the Mother of God.

Even the gospel of the first Mass in its final sentence points far beyond the birth in the manger. It is a sad and mischievous misunderstanding indeed to imagine as a simple Christmas greeting, in the style of the mummers, that striking scene of the "multi-

tude of the heavenly army" suddenly surrounding the angel who
has appeared to the shepherd and crying: "Glory to God in high
heaven, and peace on earth to men that are God's friends." This
angelic army is not just wishing God glory and men on earth
peace at Christmas! The angel message is not a wish at all; it has
none of the conditional quality of a mere wish, none of the uncertainty of the optative mood! It is a forthright statement about
the condition of the world as such and in relation to God, in
relation to the condition brought about by the birth of the Son of
God. The question for the congregation is therefore not whether
the angel's wish has in fact been fulfilled. The question is rather
whether this congregation confesses the fact that, since the Son of
God has been invested with the world, God's *doxa* has truly and
actually shone forth again in the world, that the human race in
Christ Jesus is truly united to God and in this union finds its fulfillment and its peace; in the words of the apostle: "In Christ the
whole plenitude of Deity is embodied, and dwells in him, and it
is in him that you find your completion" (Col 2, 9 f.). It would
be a most rewarding experience to preach a Christmas sermon
which would lead the congregation to realize and to profess, in
the light of the nativity of Christ in the crib, that they are indeed
in the glory of God and in peace, even amid the persecution and
strife of the world. This is precisely the demand levied upon
Christendom by the nativity of the Lord. This is the interpretation put upon the gospel in the epistle as well: The grace of God
"has dawned," has become a reality, in our Saviour, not merely
on that far-off day but for all time; and it is this grace which,
when we affirm it as an interior reality of our own lives, enables
us in this mystic rite to look "forward, blessed in our hope, to the
day when there will be a new dawn of glory, the glory of the
great God, the glory of our Saviour Jesus Christ." This passage
of the epistle makes it quite clear that the Christmas liturgy of
the Church points not only to the past, but also, like Advent, to
the future.

But the entry of the Son of God into the world is not a smooth and uncontested affair. The world is in opposition to God, in the wake of the sin of Adam. God may be said to retake possession of the world by force in the incarnation of his Son. This incarnation becomes, in the actual historical contest, a *challenge* to the forces hostile to God. This is clearly expressed in the Introit of the first Mass. God installs his Son as Lord over the world and settles accounts with his enemies. In the face of this, there is no place for any sentimentality, however blissful or pious, in hymn or sermon. This is a moment of decision, for community and for individual, in the words of the epistle, "to forego irreverent thoughts and worldly appetites, and to live, in this present world, a life of order, of justice, and of holiness."

The congregation is aware of this challenging summons. In Gradual and Alleluia verse, the worshipers look far beyond the idyllic scene of the manger. They hear the word of prophecy, testifying to the eternal generation of the Son and to the promise made to him of dominion over his enemies—again that mention of enemies!

These texts prepare the congregation for a proper inner understanding of the message of the nativity in the manger, an understanding that transcends such externals as ox and ass and straw! And so the congregation can enter with the rejoicing of the heavens and the gladness of the earth into the holy sacrifice (Offertory), for it knows itself to be experiencing here and now this coming of the Lord, of that Lord whose rising is in the brightness of the holy ones and in the radiant light of the morning-star announcing the new, everlasting day of the Lord (Communion). In the vision of this day, the Christian company of the faithful stands fast in all the changes and chances of this transitory world. The nativity of the Lord in the flesh has furnished his faithful with a firm foundation for their own unflinching steadfastness. And they pray in the Collect "that we who have known the mystery of his light on earth may also attain to his joys in heaven"; in the Secret "that through this most blessed exchange of gifts (*per haec sacrosancta commercia*) we may be conformed to him in whom our human nature is united to you"; and in the Postcommunion "that we may so bear ourselves as to be fit to share his eternal destiny."

SECOND MASS

The same principle must be followed in interpreting the second Mass of Christmas. Again the gospel presents a sober historical report, the account of the visit of the shepherds to the crib. Mary is here reported to have "treasured up all these sayings, and reflected on them in her heart." She does not appear to have mastered the mystery of the incarnation as easily as many Christian congregations today unfortunately think they have mastered it! The epistle proceeds to interpret afresh what has begun with the nativity of Christ. In it God's great love for mankind has dawned upon us: now our own works, even the best of them, are of no avail; what sustains and elevates us, what makes us truly "whole" is the mercy of God, which we have experienced in baptism as regeneration and renewal in the Holy Spirit. So does the incarnation of Christ point the way beyond the whole span of time to the inheritance of which we already take possession in him in the hope of life everlasting.

In the spirit of the dawn hour when this Mass is celebrated, its other proper texts are an expression of the joy we feel at seeing the light of which the Introit speaks. Herein we may perhaps see a last vestige of the coincidence in Rome of the feast of the nativity of our Lord with the festival of the *Sol invictus* especially sacred to the Roman legions who on that day honored Mithras, the ancient Persian god of light and enemy of the powers of darkness. Now it is we who, in the words of the Collect, "are transfused with the new light of thy incarnate Word" and who pray that this Word "may shine forth in our works which now by faith is a splendor in our minds."

In the Gradual the congregation expresses at once its tribute to the glory of this Word now come to earth and its conviction, after hearing the epistle, that baptism has indeed made every Christian "light in the Lord."

Of special importance and significance in this second Mass of Christmas is the Offertory. And this Offertory is even more curiously formulated than the Offertories of the first and third Masses: "God has made the world firm and it shall not be shaken." No one nurtured in modern Christmas piety would consider this verse "Christmasy"! But anyone who adverts to the fact that the Church has proclaimed in the Martyrologium on the Vigil of Christmas that Jesus Christ, the Father's eternal Son, is born into the world "to the end that the world might be solidified" [1] *will* understand this Offertory verse. The Son of God, who has entered into created human nature [2] and united hypostatically to himself that created human nature, is the ultimate pledge of the inviolate durability of that created human nature. The cosmological and anthropological significance of the incarnation come out with special clarity in this second Mass of Christmas. What the world is and what man is, what the world can become and what man can become is made comprehensively clear to us only by the fact that the Word has become flesh. When we receive the incarnate Word in Communion, we, the congregation, as representatives of our whole human race, are told: "Glad news for thee, widowed Sion! Cry out for happiness, Jerusalem forlorn! See where thy king comes to greet thee, a trusty deliverer." [3] Is not this the most splendid proclamation that can be pealed forth

---

[1] Cf. Col 1, 15–23—Publisher's note.

[2] The original has here "Fleisch," literally "flesh," and Pinsk's concreteness must always be taken very seriously. But here we have felt that his own point is better served by taking the word, as he also often uses it, in the Hebrew sense of the perishable as opposed to the serenely eternal ("All *flesh* is grass"; and cf. especially above p. 127ff., Pinsk's gloss of St. Paul's contraposition of "flesh" and "spirit," also the entire homily for the fifteenth Sunday after Pentecost).

[3] We have here found the Knox rendering incomparably more poignant and telling for Pinsk's own point than the mystifying and gratuitous evocation of daughters in the more familiar version, which entirely sacrifices the vital element of contrast. But in deference to the official Missal text and to the pious memories of many, we append the more familiar version: "Rejoice exceedingly, daughter of Sion, announce it abroad, O daughter of Jerusalem! Behold thy King, the Holy One and Saviour of the world, cometh to thee." —Translator's notes.

into this world of ours? But its splendor depends upon the honesty and strength of that faith with which we can and do affirm its content, in spite of calamities and in the face of worldly tyrants. Yet such an affirmation and *only* such an affirmation constitutes a proclamation of the glory of God and peace among men. This realization and *only* this realization is the convincing proof that a congregation has truly celebrated the mystery of the incarnation.

THIRD MASS

The congregation that has celebrated the nativity of the Lord in the first and second Masses of Christmas in such a way as to appreciate its true meaning and significance, can indeed join enthusiastically in the exultation of the Introit of this third Mass of Christmas. Such a congregation will indeed be keenly aware of the child born to us and the son given to us, but it will retain nothing more of that Bethlehem scene. With the eye of faith, the worshipers will see this child and this son when "upon his shoulder is supreme sovereignty" and his name is proclaimed "herald of the great decree," that decree of God proclaimed by the angels, the glory of God and the peace of all mankind. And when the congregation is urged: "Sing to the Lord a new song, for he has done wondrous deeds," this new song will be the song of the angels, the only adequate portrayal of the new status of humanity and of the world, established once and for all by the miracle of the incarnation.

The miracle of this "new birth" is our motivation in the three Prayers for imploring the special grace of Christmas. This we do most plainly in the Postcommunion, in which the Saviour of the world born this day is recognized as the author of our divine generation and invoked as the dispenser of our immortality. How deeply must the generation of Christians have grasped the mystery of the incarnation who were able to formulate such Christmas prayers! It would be instructive to compare with such fervent and meaningful prayers the petitions addressed in modern prayers to the infant in the crib. I think the modern prayers would all prove to be distressingly vague, rambling, and superficial.

A congregation which has pierced the veil of the crib and seen the incarnate Son of God, will follow with exultant and passionate interest what the epistle has to tell us about mankind in Christ Jesus. The worshipers know that this Christ is one of us, for he was carried in the germ plasm of humanity from Adam and born of a daughter of Adam. And now they hear stunning reports about him, promoting him far above the dignity of the angels: he, this "one of us," is certified as the heir of the universe; through him the worlds were made; he is the brightness of God's glory and the epiphany of God's being; he upholds all things by his enabling word; he effects man's purgation from sin; he thrones at the right hand of God's majesty, exalted above the angels. And then the epistle intones a thunderous hymn of praise to the renown of the incarnate Son of God, that very renown which is the object of our homage, as his faithful subjects, in the liturgy of this feast. This epistle must be read in an appropriate style, impressing each point upon the listeners, driving each statement home, so that the congregation may learn to see aright him who lies in the manger. Then will this enlightened congregation break out with deep conviction into the exultation of the Gradual, hymning the universality of salvation. The worshipers will not be so interested in whether "the wind did blow so cold" in the stable of Bethlehem; they will rather shout with joy that *all the ends of the earth* see the salvation of our God, that all lands sing joyfully to him, that God proclaims his salvation and his justice before the face of all peoples. And as they exultantly proclaim the Alleluia verse, they will rejoice at the blessed day that has dawned upon us and will reverently praise the Lord because he, the "great light, has descended upon the earth."

I should like to reiterate that all these considerations are much more than my own personal private inspirations. They derive from the very posture and attitude demanded by the Christmas liturgy of the Church. And much of what we get to hear and read at Christmas, if measured against this standard demanded by the Church, reveals a highly regrettable lack of understanding or really meaningful presentation of the nativity of our Lord. The chief pity is that scarcely anyone who should most especially be, is upset about this deficiency. But many of the faithful laity *are* upset, the ones who are in a position to realize what is written in the Missal of the Church, and what can reasonably be expected of the celebration of the Christmas liturgy.

If the impact of the epistle could be surpassed, then the gospel of this Mass would do just that. Here there is truly the meeting of the highest and the lowest, mentioned in a Christmas text. From the power and fullness of the triune God, the Word descends and is made flesh, so that we men may be able to receive this Son of God, and, by being born of God, become sons of God. Here the Christian preaching of this mystery culminates in the oft-repeated apophthegm of the Fathers: *He became man that we might become God.*[1] This way of putting it seems to us shocking, but that only shows our own narrow-mindedness. It is the language of the fathers, of the Church, and of the Holy Spirit, the language we often encounter in St. Paul, who tells us that God "has chosen us out, ... before the foundation of the world, ... to be his adopted children through Jesus Christ" (Eph 1, 4 f.). We encounter this language in the Church's liturgy; every day she prescribes that we make the bold, one might almost say, impudent claim upon God, "that we may be made partakers of his divinity, who deigned to become a sharer of our humanity"; now, surely this is the boldest claim that could be conceived or uttered! It is no longer a question of any gift of God but of God himself. It is God whom we desire: that is the unheard of pretension. But such a pretension can now be heard of! It is possible ever since it can be proclaimed that "the Word was made flesh." If only a pastor would pray together with his congregation in the

[1] Cf. my essay *Menschwerdung* (Incarnation), in *Schritte zur Mitte*, Recklinghausen 1957, pp. 96 ff.

bold faith of the fathers of old this prayer, which incidentally was not originally a prayer of oblation at all but a Christmas prayer. And what excellent priests and congregations must those have been who could so formulate the incarnation in their prayer! And we? We come out with something like "Holy infant, so tender and mild"!

What a strange and distressing fact it is that every time I speak along these lines in a sermon or a religious study group, people always ask: "Why have we never been told that before?" What am I to say? I believe that everyone who has not yet preached in this vein—and, of course, all those who have!—should from now on preach this stunning truth to the Christmas congregation as the essential kernel of the Christmas message. Perhaps many would be helped thereby to learn to take a drastically different view of themselves and of their world; just as the worshipers do in this Mass, when they immerse heaven and earth, the world and its fullness (Offertory and Communion verses) in the radiance and glory of the Son of God, because he has become man.

CHAPTER 53

Octave of Christmas

This Mass constitutes a genuine octave Mass. With the exception of the three Prayers and the gospel, all the texts are taken from the first or the third Mass of Christmas. Thus the congregation persists in the contemplation of the great salvation history vistas opened up to it in the incarnation of the Son of God. Every sermon should aim at recalling to the true Christmas atmosphere a congregation which has perhaps come to the House of God from more or less wild New Year's Eve parties. The recourse should again be to the liturgical texts, with a reminder of the *consecratio mundi*. The true Christmas atmosphere can be summed up briefly thus: the world is in Christ and Christ is in the world. It is into this framework that we must insert the account of the circumcision of the Lord, that event which imparts its own special note to the octave of the Nativity of the Lord. There are two crucial features: the circumcision itself and the naming of the child. Both are in a certain sense specifications of the incarnation, inasmuch as they show that the Son of God did not become simply "man" in general, but rather a man in a specific nation and people and with a definite name. This has the significance, in the first instance, of a complete social and political assimilation of the incarnate Son of God to his fellowmen. He becomes really one of them, compatriot and contemporary! The genuineness and consequentiality of the incarnation are here rendered evident. But circumcision and name-giving are mysteries in their own right, have their own salvation history significance. They point beyond any ordinary circumcision undertaken in the family circle by the father of the house.

With the circumcision, the newborn Son of God assumes the role historically assigned to the people of Israel; and here the prophetic utterances concerning the servant of Yahweh have special pertinence (Is 49–53). The striking phrase of the wife of Moses might also be here recalled, when in that night-skirmish with Yahweh she brusquely and resolutely circumcised her uncircumcised son and then said: "Now we are betrothed in blood!" (Ex 4, 24 ff.) Martin Buber points out that "it must surely be a question here of the tribe rather than of the individual. She accomplishes the act whereby the tribe as such was held by the Israelites to embody anew, each time that act was performed, its covenant with God (hence the symbolic act is performed upon the generative organ). Thus the woman effects the reconciliation." [1]

However this may be, God "made a covenant with Abraham, the covenant that ordained circumcision" (Acts 7, 8); thus covenant and circumcision are inseparably linked. The circumcision is the sign of the covenant and is as such an obligation to exclusive devotion to Yahweh, the Lord of the people of Israel. Now Paul says in his epistle to the Romans that "I would remind those that are circumcised that Christ came to relieve their needs; God's fidelity demanded it; he must make good his promises to our fathers" (Rom 15, 8); this means that Christ has assumed the responsibility for the fulfillment of the covenant and his circumcision is the sign of this. The covenant is concluded in blood and consummated in blood. The words of Sephora, "betrothed in

---

[1] M. Buber, *Moses*, Heidelberg [2] 1952, p. 68 ff. P. Heinisch has still another interpretation of the scene in his commentary on Exodus in the Bonn Bible of 1934; and other interpretations are also possible. For my own part, I should like to make a cautious observation in connection with the last sentence of the passage from Buber cited above: the fact is that the feast of the circumcision has from most ancient times figured as a feast of our Lady. In this Mass of the octave, unlike the three Masses *in nativitate*, there are express references to the Blessed Virgin in the Collect and Postcommunion.

blood," establish the nexus between the circumcision and the death
of the Lord on the cross. The expression "betrothed in blood" is
a familiar one to us even today as applied to the dying Lord who
sheds his blood for us, because that blood is the nuptial pledge of
the love that weds him to us, the race he came to redeem. It is
not the feast of his nativity but only the octave of that feast which
makes it clear that Jesus is really resolved to fulfill the covenant
with the shedding of his blood. But the mystery of the circumcision,
like every one of his mystico-sacramental actions, reaches beyond
the historical destiny of Jesus and is effected in us. Thus we read:
"As for circumcision, it is we who practise it, we who serve God
with the spirit and take pride in Christ Jesus" (Phil 3, 3); and
in still clearer terms: "In him you have been circumcised with a
circumcision that was not man's handiwork. It was effected, not
by despoiling the natural body, but by Christ's circumcision; you
by baptism have been united with his burial ... God raised him
from the dead. And in giving life to him, he gave life to you too,
when you lay dead in your sins, with nature all uncircumcised in
you. He condoned all your sins; cancelled the deed which excluded us ..." (Col 2, 11–14).

This passage could be considered as the classical evidence in
the matter of the mystery of the circumcision. In a much more
perfect fashion than the Israelite by the removal of the foreskin
of his body was sequestered from the world of the gentiles and
made a member of God's chosen people, does the Christian in
the burial of baptism depart from the kingdom of this world.
Baptism is indeed an even more painful operation than circumcision; the New Testament compares to death the separation from
this world therewith connected. But both baptism and circumcision initiate man into that relationship of grace with God, whose
consummation is the New Covenant, manifest in the blood of
Christ even as early as his circumcision.

This nexus becomes the more intelligible when we remember
that uncircumcision is understood in Scripture in a sense that
transcends the physical condition and signifies a lack, even if not

always a culpable lack, of the interior union with God which is demanded. Thus, Moses confesses before Yahweh that he is "of uncircumcised lips" and therefore cannot proclaim God's message (Ex 6, 12. 30). And later Yahweh proclaims through the prophets: "The whole world is uncircumcised; all have hearts uncircumcised, and Israel with the rest" (Jer 9, 25 f.). This reproach is taken up by St. Stephen in his great speech to the Sanhedrin, in which he accuses his own Jewish accusers of being "still uncircumcised in heart and ears" (Acts 7, 51). Similarly Paul recognizes as effective circumcision only that which "is achieved in the heart, according to the spirit, not the letter of the law" (Rom 2, 29).

Precisely these last modes of expression show that external circumcision is not enough, that true circumcision is achieved only when the covenant people of Old and New Testament alike free themselves from the world and dedicate themselves entirely to the service of God, to his vocation.

The congregation celebrating the mystery of the circumcision of the Lord and acknowledging this circumcision to be the sign of the real salvific intent of Jesus, must thus take very seriously, in the light of the words of St. Paul from the letter to the Colossians, the question of whether the Christian worshipers constituting this congregation are so incorporating themselves into the circumcision of the Lord; for only if they do will the incarnation of the Son of God signify for them salvation. Anyone who is delighted at the fact of the incarnation but still unwilling to accomplish the circumcision that consists in *the cutting away of the integument of this world* can derive no benefit from the incarnation. The circumcision is truly the octave, that is, the fulfillment of the nativity. Anyone celebrating the nativity but not the circumcision fails to attain to the fullness of life, which consists not in the biological process but rather in the covenant with God; and it costs blood! This makes it especially patent how totally the cozy, homey middle-class perversion of Christmas misses the point of the real salvific event.

The *name-giving* also has its salvation history significance. And this lies not merely in the fact that the name Jesus means "Saviour." Rather it is to be found in the fact that the infinite and incomprehensible God can now be identified and comprehended by a human name. This is a further proof of the consequentiality of God in the matter of the incarnation. The Son of God does not hide in an inaccessible and impenetrable anonymity. He appears as one among many on the roads of Palestine and can be summoned and "placed" by anyone. If a boy on one of the squares of Nazareth calls "Jesus!" then the incarnate Son of God will stop, because he cannot and will not deny his own name. This apparently trivial example has a far-reaching import, spanning the whole of history. Even today, the incarnate Son of God, throning exalted at the right hand of the Father, cannot deny his human name; if individual or community really call him, he will be there! Therein lies the ultimate and best theological foundation of the effectiveness of the brief ejaculatory prayers (indulgenced or not!) often consisting in nothing more than pronouncing the name of God or Jesus.

After Yahweh had revealed his name to Moses in the burning bush, Israel could call upon him. This invocation has nothing in common with magic, for God had revealed his name to his people out of love, as the everlasting pledge of his love. Again and again we hear God say in Scripture: "Mine it is to rescue him; he acknowledges my name...when he calls upon me, I will listen" (Ps 90, 14–15). This invocation is not just any sort of calling out of God's name; it is a summoning of him to us and it results in the *adesse* of God. God is there; he stands by us. Not as a mere bystander but as one who truly stands by his suppliant. When the liturgy teaches us to pray *adesto Domine!* the implication is always a summons to a personal compresence. The same is true of Christ, whenever we summon him by name. Of course the prerequisite is that we use more than our vocal cords and our human minds, for "only through the Holy Spirit can anyone say Jesus is the Lord" (1 Cor 21, 3).

We ought therefore to be conscious of the grace that is ours in having the name of Jesus, so to speak, placed at our disposal, as covenant people of the New Testament, so that we can establish the kingdom of God in that name and in that name repulse the enemies of God's kingdom. This great joy in the name of Jesus should be our legacy from this feast and we ought to enjoy with gratitude our power in the use of this name when we celebrate his sacraments and are enabled to offer in the power of his name his own eucharistic sacrifice to the Father. Much could also be said about this effective utilization of the name of God and Jesus Christ from the standpoint of the second commandment. There is no need whatever to try to encompass all this material in every Mass of the octave of Christmas. Circumcision, covenant, and name-giving could quite well be treated separately and the proper handling of any one of these great spiritual realities would arrive at and lead others to a concrete vision of the mystery of the incarnation. On occasion, the homily could treat of the community of the Jewish and Christian messianic expectation. For the circumcised Jesus is also the crucified and risen Jesus, who will come again to establish as a kingdom his Old Testament and New Testament covenant people alike. One thing only should be forbidden: to conceal the grandeur of these mysteries behind the shimmering curtain of a "New Year's Sermon"!

CHAPTER 54

Feast of the Epiphany

The Greek word *epiphaneia* from which "epiphany" is derived in classical Greek meant the appearance of the gods upon this earth. But its principal meaning in later Roman and Byzantine times is the arrival, the visit of the Caesar, of the emperor in the cities and provinces of the *Imperium Romanum*. We must use this as the basis for our understanding of today's Mass.

The simple and sober account given in today's gospel of the arrival of the magi from the East clearly points up the hegemony of the child "born king of the Jews" over all the peoples of the earth. He is in fact Lord of the world. The magi from the East do homage to him on behalf of the gentiles. The fact that his own people know him from the testimony of the prophets and are aware of his existence yet allow him to be persecuted by the earthly royal ruler who seeks to kill him—all of this cannot stay the triumphal progress of the true King of Israel.

It is a wonderful picture that Isaias paints in the reading of today's Mass. Jerusalem shines in the full radiance of festal illumination, which is but an external sign of the interior light and the glory that is dawning in this city because its king has come; this light rises the more brilliantly upon Jerusalem because all the world around is covered in darkness and gloom, lying in the primordial chaos. Only Jerusalem, city of God and of his envoy, blazes with light which spreads from her over all the peoples of the earth. It is a stunning vision, this pilgrimage of the sons and daughters of Jerusalem and of the peoples of the whole earth to this true center of the world and of God's glory upon earth. Jerusalem's absorption of all the glories of the world highlights still more clearly and convincingly the power of her king. This Jerusalem is not the old Jerusalem in Palestine; it is the new Jerusalem coming down from heaven whose provisional mold is the *Church* of Jesus Christ. What a panorama of human history!

The congregation remains enthralled by this vision, in which it recognizes *itself!* The worshipers meditate in the Gradual with pious and reverent amazement the words, "All the men of Saba with their gifts of gold and incense, their cry of praise to the Lord! Rise up, Jerusalem, and shine forth! Thy dawn is come, the glory of the Lord breaks upon thee!" This meditation is also an admonition to the Christian community of our day to engrave deep upon its heart this picture of the glory of Christ the King and of his city and to preserve it with reverent care.

Certainly the vision proclaimed in today's reading has not yet been consummated. But this vision is no mere figment of the imagination, no utopian invention. Its realization in the course of history began with the event reported in the gospel. Even though the glory of the Lord remained for the moment hidden in that event of the arrival of the magi, nonetheless that event constituted a beginning leading to the final consummation and fulfillment of which the epistle speaks. Toward this fulfillment the course of history presses forward with the compelling impetus provided by the Word of the Lord of history, God's anointed envoy, vanquisher of every contending force.

This consummation is pledged by the mighty word of the Lord of Hosts: "I am God, and there is no other, none to rival me; did I not tell you from the first the events of latter days, from the beginning what had not yet come to be? My purpose, I promised, should not fail, my whole will must needs be done...I, that spoke, will make my word good; I, that purposed it, will accomplish my purpose" (Is 46, 10 ff.). "Keep yourself unsullied, you that have the vessels of the Lord's worship in your charge. No need for confusion at the time of your going; this shall be no hasty flight, with the Lord himself to march before you, the God of Israel to rally you" (Is 52, 11–12).

Within this stream of history lies also the feast of the Epiphany, recurring on the sixth day of the first month of every year; retrospectively linked with the homage of the magi and pointing forward to the confluence of the peoples striving toward the radiance of the king in his holy city. Thus does epistle interpret gospel and gospel pledge the realization of the vision of epistle.

The community of worshipers is incorporated into the very sequence of events here being celebrated. When the worshipers assemble to do their homage and service to their king, that king himself holds solemn entry among them and they celebrate his arrival with pious and reverent amazement. So is the Introit to be understood: "Behold, the Lord, the Ruler, appears [the Latin *advenit* has exactly the same special significance as the Greek verb *epiphanein*] and the kingdom is in his hand and power and dominion." So does the company of worshipers see its Christ in this Mass. The worshipers see themselves in this public assembly as the legitimate successors of the magi of old who "have seen his star in the East and have come to worship him." The fact that the Gradual adds the phrase "with gifts" and the Communion verse repeats this addition is an especially poignant proof that the Church authorizes the community assembled for the holy mysteries and offering the holy gifts to consider itself as performing the identical service that the magi performed to the identical Lord.

Still more clearly does the congregation express its conviction of being representative of the whole world when, during the Offertory, it recites or sings the Psalm verse: "The kings of Tharsis and the isles shall offer gifts, the kings of Arabia and Saba shall bring tribute. All kings shall pay him homage, all nations shall serve him," precisely in the service and homage of the faithful who go up to the altar of the Lord with their gifts.

The Christian worshipers who structured the celebration of this feast in this way showed thereby that they had a conception of the dignity of the royal priesthood accruing to them from their vocation to the service of the Lord. This feast therefore becomes the true feast of the kingship of Christ, a world-wide radiant kingship filling mankind with glory. It is striking that so few pious edifying phrases are to be found in this Mass text. The sentences of the epistle rather represent a concatenation of *political* formulations and conceptions. And the other texts align themselves to this bias. This is a matter worthy of attention. This feast aims not so much at a representation of virtues and pious exhortations as rather at a portrayal of the great triumph awaiting God's politic in the ultimate structuring of his world. Him the community of worshipers regard with shining eyes, by him they are enthralled, as they confess the glory of Christ the king. They also know that the Lord will not fail to lead his kingdom to final victory in the face of the political and human chaos now seething in our time.

With its celebration of the Epiphany of the Lord, the Christian community of worshipers places itself in this kingdom and so even now takes possession of its glory. The worshipers have but one plea, that they may behold with unclouded vision and enjoy eternally what they have here celebrated in this mystic office. If this radiant feast conceals a warning, it is this: the Church of Jesus Christ has to understand, even in times of anguish and affliction, that the glory of the Lord fills her with radiance and she has the duty of witnessing to this glory of her Lord before all the peoples of the earth, with no anxious concern, no cowardly fear, no squinting sidelong glances after the securities and bail-bonds of this world!

CHAPTER 55

Feast of the Holy Family

The Mass of the feast of the holy family takes the place of the Mass of the Sunday within the octave of the Epiphany on the first Sunday after Epiphany. This Mass of the feast retains only the gospel from this former Mass of the Sunday within the octave. This gospel sheds upon the much more modest feast of the holy family the radiance of the feast of the Epiphany. For the account of the boy Jesus in the temple is an epiphany account, inasmuch as it reports a flashing forth from the boy of his own awareness of his absolute divine sovereignty both in relation to the doctors of the law and in relation to his own parents. He reveals his hieratic majesty with that sentence that bursts all the bounds of bourgeois family feeling: I must needs be in the place that belongs to my Father!—a saying which Mary and Joseph did not understand, so lofty were its implications. But this does not prevent both Sunday gospel and feast-day gospel from adding: "But he went down with them on their journey to Nazareth, and lived there in subjection to them."

The two poles of the absolute sovereignty claimed and the patient obedience accorded provide the basis for the mysterious *tension* of the Christian family. The Christian family is not exclusively a biologico-tribal entity as are the families of other cultures. The real essence of the Christian family would therefore not be comprehended by any sermon for this feast day which attempted to place in the foreground the natural factors and features of natural family life, however fine and meaningful these may be. This essence of the Christian family lies rather that in it Christ and his kingdom can really be established. This was true, to a certain extent, even of the family of the Old Testament covenant people. The promise of the fourth commandment, "so thou shalt live long to enjoy the land which the Lord thy God means to give thee" (Ex 20, 12) obviously means that, in the final analysis, the Jewish family is not directed simply to the establishment of a cultural tribal or national pattern, as, say, the Athenian or Roman family, or in our own days the American family true to its own best traditions; rather, the Jewish family is the colony and instrument for the preparation of the kingdom of the Messiah. This is a status quite different from that of the family in classical or western culture. The same is true, to an even greater degree, of the Christian family which is therefore sometimes called an *ecclesiola* a Church in microcosm. It would be better to say that the mystery of the Christian family lies in the fact that it is the cell in which the kingdom of God germinates throughout history.

The ultimate goal is not therefore to use the slogan of the "Christian family" to shore up and secure traditional family customs and mores against changing times and cultural patterns, nor yet to overwork the fourth commandment for the same purpose. It is rather to assure that in one way or another (and the fashion may vary in function of the cultural or social level of the individual family) the words of the epistle for this feast will be fulfilled in every Christian family: that the members will again learn to understand that they are "God's chosen ones, holy and beloved"; that they will create out of this burgeoning realization an atmosphere of love and peace, not deriving from bourgeois placidity but rather from the joy in the love and peace of Christ; and, above all, that their conversation shall be of Christ and his work and that they shall speak with gratitude and joy, precisely against the background of the misery of the world. Only such a pattern can mold the *de facto* familial life of parents and children into *de jure* Christian family living. The mystery of the "hidden king, the God of Israel, the Saviour" ought to be discussed in the family circle; not in pseudoecstasy nor pious pose, not with eyes rolled heavenward nor in sepulchral tones, but quietly and naturally, with the parents giving the children to understand that they cannot themselves explain the great mystery of their family nor interpret it for them but that it is there nonetheless, as sheerest reality, even without any apparitions! Then will that great mystery shine forth not only in the house of Nazareth but in every home where the community of the people of Christ is borne through the ages. And the Christian home will become the image of "the house of the Lord" (Gradual), a joy to all who live in it and a center for the radiation into the world of the glory of God.

The holy family of Nazareth must not remain simply a moral model; in this respect it would be outmoded in many ways and the new look, after the invasion of that family by the divine claim, would go almost unnoticed. The holy family is an allegorical symbol, a mystery that is prolonged and reproduced in every Christian family, permeating every aspect, including the ties of the sexual union.

A poignant note in this Mass, worthy of special attention, is the perfect dovetailing of Offertory and Communion verses. The Christian family, in its Offertory procession, brings itself, with everything that it is and has, as a cell of the mystical body of Christ to be incorporated now into the eucharistic sacrifice; its reward is the reception of the eucharistic body of Christ enabling it to live still more in his radiance and his glory, in his love and his peace, even in the midst of a strife-torn outside world. But in the midst of the Christian family is Christ. Christian family living consists simply in the positive expression of this reality in every aspect of family life. Without this positive expression of the interior reality of Christ, the family may well be entirely respectable, even good and wise, even indeed to a certain extent meritorious in the sight of God; but an existential Christian family it is not!

CHAPTER 56

Second Sunday after Epiphany

Of the three great events which are expressly combined in the feast of the Epiphany on January 6 [1]—the arrival of the magi, the baptism of Jesus in the Jordan and the changing of the water into wine at Cana—the Church on this Sunday celebrates in a special way the third, namely "this first of his signs [which] Jesus worked at Cana of Galilee." The epiphanic nature of this event comes out in the last sentence of the gospel passage read at Mass today: "...and he manifested his glory and his disciples believed in him." This sentence therefore should also furnish the real theme of the liturgical homily, which must abstract from the other important and interesting circumstances which should be treated in a biblical homily.

We shall have to consider carefully wherein the manifestation of glory actually consisted, or better, what was the reason that the disciples became so overwhelmingly aware of that glory that they "believed in him" and what element of this event was the actual object of their faith. The miracle occurred entirely unobtrusively, after all: not a single word or gesture of Jesus effecting the miracle is reported. On the contrary, it is expressly stated that

[1] Pinsk is here evidently referring to the Office (cf. Antiphon to *Magnificat* of second Vespers): "We solemnize a day adorned with three miracles [this, without prejudice to Pinsk's strongly made point below, is the only possible rendition of the Latin "miraculis"]: today a star led the magi to the crib; today wine was made out of water at a marriage feast; today Christ was baptized, at his own request, by John in Jordan, that he might save us. Alleluia."—Translator's note.

only the servants who had drawn the water knew and no one else. The statement "he manifested his glory" must therefore surely have reference to something transcending the modest external course of the miracle, since after all the chief steward, even after tasting the good wine, is not reported to have altered his opinion of Jesus in the least; he seems to have regarded the whole affair and the person of Jesus entirely from the standpoint of his own professional concerns. Nor are the other wedding guests reported to have been moved by this manifestation of his glory to believe in Jesus; the only thing reported is that "his disciples believed in him."

Now it seems to me that all of these circumstances require serious attention. John never speaks in his gospel of the words of Jesus as miracles (*terata*), but always as signs (*semeia*). And so the changing of the water into wine is not the first "miracle" that Jesus worked, but rather "the beginning of the signs." Jesus uses signs in the same way as parables, so that men "seeing may not see and hearing may not hear or understand" (Mt 13, 13). And the sign likewise can be seen by all without its meaning, the meaning Jesus intended it to have, being at once understood by everyone. But to the disciples "it is given to understand the secrets of God's kingdom" (Mt 13, 11). We shall therefore be compelled to assume that Jesus revealed the meaning of the sign here to the disciples in some special way, that he manifested to them and only to them perhaps in his own person something of the brilliant radiance of his Godhead, so that the disciples all at once saw him with quite different eyes, even as did Peter after the miraculous catch of fishes, when he could only stammer: "Leave me to myself, Lord . . . I am a sinner" (Lk 5, 8).

Thus did the disciples learn that in Jesus they were dealing with superhuman greatness and they believed in him as the one who would bring the Kingdom of God. It is difficult to say to what extent this revelation also made clear to them the hidden meaning of the miracle of transmutation in Cana. But the Church makes this hidden meaning clear in her liturgy. We need only meditate attentively on the magnificent words of the homily of St. Augustine on this gospel, appearing in the Breviary, to grasp the nexus between a wedding feast (even the most modest family gathering) and the redemptive ministry of Jesus Christ, which is substantially nothing other than the *marriage of the Lamb* with redeemed humanity, a true marriage feast, a true nuptial banquet, union of divine and human life in mutually beatifying love, round that festal board at which is served the good wine of eternal happiness, "kept ... until now." Once this nexus has been grasped, then it is easy to understand that the Mass of this Sunday is likewise a "sign" rendering accessible to us the consummate joy of our nuptials with the celestial bridegroom. Indeed the Communion rite is today accompanied by the words of the chief steward: "Thou hast kept the good wine until now." In the sacred mysteries of this Sunday, Jesus works the sign as once in Cana; and we, as his disciples, recognize therein his glory and enter, full of faith, into loving and joyous communion with him.

This is what should dawn upon the congregation today; then that congregation would see a genuine manifestation of God's glory in the words of the epistle concerning the manifold riches of the faithful; and the worshipers would realize, with overflowing gratitude, that this glory is in each one of them, even if often hidden, and that it is only waiting for Christians to give it a place in their life. Of such high mysteries this Mass should convey at least a hint.

Then the Epiphany exultation pervading Introit, Gradual, Alleluia verse and Offertory will be easy to understand. The "sign" of Jesus must become intelligible to the congregation and impel every member to a faith in him like that shown by the disciples. Only such a community of worshipers will be able to exult in this fashion, not only in times of earthly good fortune but also in times of grim affliction. All of us priests who are privileged to celebrate such a liturgy with our congregations should regard it as a rewarding duty to achieve this objective.

CHAPTER 57

Third Sunday after Epiphany

A stunning gesture opens this Sunday's liturgy: the human community invites the angels to worship God and delights and exults in this glorification of God. But can this gesture of the Church and her summons to the angels be taken seriously? Well, anyone inclined to consider the words of the Introit to be extravagant phrases, devoid of objective legitimacy or justification, should read what Paul has to reveal, "The principalities and powers of heaven are to see, now, made manifest in the Church, the subtlety of God's wisdom" (Eph 3, 10); and further what St. Peter says of the wonderful tidings that are revealed in the Holy Spirit through the gospel, "And now the angels can satisfy their eager gaze; the Holy Spirit has been sent ... your evangelists have made the whole mystery plain to you instead" (1 Pt 1, 12).

There is nothing exaggerated or out of place in the human community of worshipers who have truly celebrated Epiphany and in this way experienced the manifestation of God's glory in his mysteries, shouting its joy and pride over what God has wrought for his faithful ones on earth so that the echo rings to the very borders of the universe.

A like joy and exultation permeates all the Propers of the Mass of this Sunday and the coming Sundays after Epiphany. They set a quite clear-cut assignment for priest and congregation: that of cultivating an intimate and familiar *joy in the glory of God*, in the Church. We moderns tend to boggle at such thoughts and sentiments. We are sooner ready to believe in our sinfulness and wretchedness, in the miserable consequences of our misdeeds and shortcomings, and we are often shy about admitting that God displays in us stupendous glories notwithstanding, which we subsume under the title of Epiphany. Yet we must admit this, if indeed we want to understand what we are as a Church.

Today's gospel initiates us into such an attitude. The story of the centurion and his servant is familiar to us in all its details and the "Lord, I am not worthy . . ." is almost too familiar! But it seems to me that one point in this passage is often overlooked: the fact that Jesus marvels at the faith of the centurion!

Is it not nearly incomprehensible that Jesus would be joyously surprised by a man's faith? To be sure, the centurion's profession of faith has been preceded by a kind of Epiphany on the part of Jesus; but the centurion's faith remains a cause for admiration notwithstanding. Is not the same thing true of the worshiping community on this Sunday? The worshipers are confronted with Jesus, hidden in a sense in his word and his sacrament; and they surmount all objections and all temptations from without and within to profess this Jesus their Lord. Not by their own unaided power, of course! But because to them is granted the grace to understand his "sign." Gazing as they do upon the content of this sign, the faithful can reveal it to the angels and summon them to worship the mystery of the incarnation, in which worship the faithful themselves then join with exultation and gratitude. (Special stress should be laid in this context upon the Sanctus.) From the epistle the congregation knows how the epiphany of the Lord is to affect each of its members.

And when the congregation met for worship has grasped all of this, then it will incorporate itself unreservedly into the sacrifice of the Lord, knowing, in an ultimate certainty of faith, that "the right hand of the Lord has exercised power; the right hand of the Lord has lifted me up. I shall not die, but live, and shall declare the works of the Lord" (Offertory). And when the worshipers have received the body of the Lord, they fall into speechless amazement at what they have been privileged to learn from the ministry of the Lord about this world and the next, about God and themselves, at "these things that came from the mouth of God" (Communion verse), *now*, during this Mass.

CHAPTER 58

Fourth Sunday after Epiphany

The Epiphany exultation of the congregation is mixed today with the growling of a storm in both the Scripture readings.

The quieting of the storm at sea is here reported by St. Matthew, but a deeper understanding is promoted by incorporating the reports from the gospel according to St. Mark and that according to St. Luke as well (Mk 4, 35–41; Lk 8, 22–25). A sudden squall of rain driven by a blustering wind hits the lake, lashing the water into towering waves that break threateningly over the boat. Deadly danger for the vessel! Sheer panic seizes the passengers! All but one, that is; "meanwhile, he was in the stern, asleep on the pillow there" (Mk 4, 38). Divine calm and sovereign serenity in the midst of the tumult of the elements and the abject terror of the disciples who wake him with the reproachful question: "Master, art thou unconcerned? We are sinking!" (Mk 4, 38).

A typical human non sequitur, this! Predicated on the false premise that there is only one possible solution in any situation. Would they have sunk, then, if they had let the master sleep on? Was it necessary for Jesus to get up in order to avert the danger? Is it not enough for Jesus to be there, even asleep?

But he does get up. And now there comes a striking passage: "He ... checked the wind, and said to the sea: 'Peace, be still!'" The original Greek word here translated "be still" means literally "stop (or shut) your mouth!" and was used in exorcisms. So Jesus is treating the threatening squall and the sea it has lashed to foam as if they were demoniacs!

The demons ravish not only men but nature as well. For the sin of man has plunged nature as well into the power of the devil, whose name in Greek is *diabolos*, the addler, the muddler. He it is who attempts to exploit the sin of man to plunge the world into chaos, after having destroyed the harmony of the universe through the sin of Adam. But Jesus is "the Saviour of the world" who makes not only man but all material nature truly "whole" in the last great epiphany of the "new heaven and the new earth." The quieting of the storm at sea is a symbolic preview of that eschatological epiphany. This is shown by the remark of the evangelist, "and there was deep calm."

To the disciples, the Lord addresses a rebuke no less stern than the one he has flung at the rebellious elements. "What cowards you are!" he chides them, "Where is your faith?" Cowardice is the culmination of disbelief. Therefore the cowards are mentioned in first place among the damned in the Apocalypse, before the murderers, the fornicators, the poisoners, the idolators and the liars (Ap 21, 8). But this stern rebuke is the prelude to his epiphany: the disciples are overcome with awe and their question, though it still betrays confusions clearly indicates the resurgence of their faith: "What manner of man is this, that even the wind and the sea obey him?"

In the storm, therefore, does the Lord reveal his glory and it is mirrored in the smooth radiance of the sea. The disciples are restored to the clear light of faith which—even if perhaps only for the moment—banishes their physical terror and mental anguish. Again it is epiphany: he reveals his glory!

As echo of the gospel, the epistle can also justifiably be called "stormy" in a certain sense. For the short categorical imperative sentences of this passage from the letter to the Romans graphically evoke the stormy breakers of the passions that lash every human soul so fiercely as to rouse sheer terror that they will swamp it. And how often God keeps silence in such hours of anguish and affliction, how often Christ sleeps even as the soul totters in mortal peril! We must not, therefore, read the epistle as a series of moral precepts; rather we must try to put it in the context of the gospel and sense the *demonic powers* it evokes, those powers to whom we are all exposed, each in his own way.

But in this stormy epistle, likewise, there is the epiphany: *love.* The love that we have showered upon us by God at all times and in all places, whether he wakes or sleeps, whether he keeps silence or speaks. This love of God is bestowed upon us in his Spirit, the breath of his life, "who is poured out into our hearts." In the strength of this love, then, lies the calm amid the storm, for "love...is the fulfillment of the law." Our certainty that that love will not fail us enables us to exult today, as we have done on all the Sundays after Epiphany, even though the storm still rages all about us.